Group Problem Solving

Group Problem Solving

Patrick R. Laughlin

PRINCETON UNIVERSITY PRESS

PRINCETON AND OXFORD

Published by Princeton University Press, 41 William Street, Princeton, New Jersey 08540
In the United Kingdom: Princeton University Press, 6 Oxford Street, Woodstock,
Oxfordshire OX20 1TW
press.princeton.edu

Library of Congress Cataloging-in-Publication Data

Laughlin, Patrick R., 1934–
Group problem solving / Patrick R. Laughlin.
p. cm.
Includes bibliographical references and index.
ISBN 978-0-691-14790-1 (hbk. : alk. paper) — ISBN 978-0-691-14791-8 (pbk. : alk.
paper) 1. Group problem solving. 2. Small groups. 3. Problem solving. I. Title.
HD30.29.L38 2011
658.4'036—dc22
2010030839

British Library Cataloging-in-Publication Data is available

This book has been composed in Sabon

Printed on acid-free paper. ∞

Printed in the United States of America

10 9 8 7 6 5 4 3 2 1

To Rosemary

CONTENTS

LIST OF FIGURES

LIST OF TABLES

ACKNOWLEDGMENTS

I THANK Editor Eric Schwartz and Rita Bernhard, Janie Y. Chan, Leslie Flis, and Leslie Grundfest of Princeton University Press—it has been a pleasure to work with them.

Some tables and illustrations have been adapted, redrawn, or derived from versions previously published as articles in the journals *Group Processes and Intergroup Relations*, *Journal of Experimental Social Psychology*, *Journal of Personality and Social Psychology*, and *Organizational Behavior and Human Decision Processes*.

I thank Harold R. Carey for his many contributions.

Group Problem Solving

Chapter One

BASIC CONCEPTS IN GROUP PROBLEM SOLVING

IN THE MOST GENERAL SENSE, a problem is a discrepancy between a current less desirable state and a future more desirable state. The current state may be a simple question such as "Who was the first President of the United States" and the desired state the answer "George Washington." The current state may be the diameter of a circle and the desired state the circumference of the circle. The current state may be a set of clues in a crossword puzzle and the desired state the correct answers. The current state may be a new deadly contagious disease and the desired state an understanding of the etiology, vectors, treatment, and prevention of the disease.

Although problems vary widely in domain (scientific, engineering, business and financial, artistic and literary, etc.), complexity (simple or complicated), specification (well defined or poorly defined), and relationship to other problems in a larger system, all problems involve proceeding by a series of permissible logical, mathematical, scientific, physical, or linguistic operations from the current less desirable state to the future more desirable state. Scientific research teams, auditing teams, grand juries, criminal and civil juries, university hiring committees, school boards, weather forecasters, the Council of Economic Advisors, and forensic art experts are some of the many groups who attempt to solve problems in our increasingly complex and interdependent world.

GROUP TASK, STRUCTURE, PROCESS, AND PRODUCT

Group problem solving may be analyzed in terms of four basic constructs: (a) group task, (b) group structure, (c) group process, and (d) group product. The group *task* is what the group is attempting to do. *Group structure* is the organization of the group, including (a) *roles*, the different positions within the group, (b) *norms*, the expected beliefs and behaviors for the group members, and (c) *member characteristics*, the demographic, physical, and psychological attributes of each group member. *Group process* is how the group members interact with and influence one another. *Group product* is the collective group response or output. The correspondence of the product to the objective of the group defines success or failure and determines the rewards or punishments for the group members. In *cooperative interaction* such as group problem solving all group members have the same goal or objective and share equally in the rewards and punishments. In *mixed-motive* interaction such as social dilemmas the group members have different objectives, and the rewards and punishments vary for the different group members.

To illustrate these four constructs consider the Supreme Court of the United States. After accepting a case in the certiorari process the group task is to issue a decision with an accompanying explanation. The structure of the Court consists of the roles of Chief Justice and eight Associate Justices, all of whom serve for life unless impeached and convicted by Congress. Member characteristics are the demographic attributes and experience of each Justice such as age and gender, college and law school, and Appellate Court positions, and their knowledge, beliefs, attitudes, and values. The Court follows norms such as sitting in seniority order when the Court is hearing a case. The Chief Justice may assign other norms such as speaking in turn in seniority order without interruption during conference meetings.

After a decision to accept a case the first part of the group process involves hearing the case in open session in the Supreme Court Building, when advocates of the two parties in the case present their oral arguments and answer questions from the Justices. The Justices subsequently discuss the case in private and make a preliminary group decision by a formal vote with a simple 5/9 majority rule. If the Chief Justice is in the majority faction, he or she writes the opinion or assigns it to one of the other Associate Justices in the majority faction to write the opinion of the Court. If the Chief Justice is in the minority faction, the most senior Associate Justice in the majority faction assigns the case to one of the Associate Justices in the majority faction to write the opinion of the Court. The written opinion is then circulated among the Justices, who may respond in written agreements or dissents and suggested changes. They may discuss them with one or more other Justices. Each Justice has three or four Clerks who are also involved in writing and vetting the opinions. Subsequently the Justices meet in private for a final decision by a formal vote with a 5/9 simple majority rule.

The final group product is a Supreme Court Decision with the accompanying written majority opinion, perhaps with further statements by both the concurring Justices and the dissenting Justices explaining their individual reasoning. Greenburg (2007) and Toobin (2007) present informative and interesting accounts of the individual Justices, procedures, policies, decisions, and controversies of competing interest groups and congressional parties in the Supreme Court under Chief Justices Rehnquist and Roberts. Amar (2005) presents a comprehensive history of the U.S. Constitution and the steadily increasing importance of the

Supreme Court in interpreting the Constitution and the constitutionality of federal and state laws.

INTERPERSONAL INFLUENCE PROCESSES

In a classic chapter French and Raven (1969) distinguished five types of interpersonal influence processes, or power. *Reward power* is the capacity of the group members to provide desirable experiences and outcomes for one another, whereas *coercive power* is the capacity of the group members to provide undesirable experiences and outcomes for one another. In the Supreme Court the Chief Justice assigns opinions to the other Justices, and thus is able to reward or punish them by the number and desirability of assignments. *Expert power* derives from specialized knowledge and abilities, training, and experience. On the Supreme Court the Justices vary in their knowledge and experience in specific areas of the law and past constitutional history, and hence have corresponding expert power over the other Justices. *Legitimate power* derives from a formal system that is accepted by the group members and the larger society. The legitimate power of the Justices to determine the meaning of the law and decide cases follows from their nomination by the President and approval by the Senate. Finally, *referent power* derives from identification with a respected person or institution. The Justices typically identify strongly with one another and with the Supreme Court as an institution, although they may not agree on judicial philosophy, values, or particular cases (Greenburg 2007).

More generally, these five types of interpersonal influence or power may be aggregated as *informational influence* and *normative influence* (Deutsch and Gerard 1955). In *informational influence* group members influence one another by information about people, abstract systems, and world knowledge. In *normative influence* group members influence one another by rewards, punishments, norms, and values. Basically informational influence concerns matters of truth, and normative influence concerns matters of value. The long history of theories of attitudes in social psychology may be considered attempts to integrate matters of truth and matters of value in the single construct of attitude (Eagly and Chaikin 1993; McGuire 1969, 1985).

GROUP TASKS

Additive, Compensatory, Conjunctive, Disjunctive, and Complementary

In a seminal article Steiner (1966) proposed five types of group tasks. *Additive* tasks are situations in which all group members perform individually and the group product is the sum of the member products. For example, a number of employees in a large office may each independently process applications for credit cards without interacting with one another. The group product is the sum of the applications processed individually by each of the employees. On *compensatory* tasks all group members estimate some current or future quantity or event, without any group interaction, and the group product is the mean or median of the individual estimates. For example, a number of stockbrokers may estimate the value of the Dow Jones Industrial Index one year in the future, and the group product is computed as the mean of their individual estimations. The best-selling book *The Wisdom of Crowds* (Surowiecki 2004) gives many examples of compensatory tasks.

In contrast to additive and compensatory tasks, where the group members do not interact with one another, on conjunctive, disjunctive, and complementary tasks the group members interact with one another and influence one another to produce a group product. On a *conjunctive* group task all group members must succeed in order for the group to succeed. Examples include a group of mountain climbers roped together, where a single member who falls will bring disaster to all, or a rowing team, where a single member who "pulls a crab" will result in group failure. On a *disjunctive* group task, the group will succeed if a single group member succeeds. An example is a small group of high school students working on an algebra problem, where one group member who knows the correct answer persuades the others to accept it as the group response. Conjunctive and disjunctive tasks are thus the end points of a continuum of the number of group members who must succeed for the group to succeed. Other group tasks require that fewer than all group members or more than one member must succeed for group success. For example, in a cross-country meet each team may enter seven runners, but only the first five finishers count for the team score.

A *complementary* group task allows the group members to combine different abilities, skills, knowledge, or other physical and cognitive resources in a collective product that is more than any group member could produce alone. Examples include coordinated group tasks such as a football team running a play or an orchestra performing a symphony. A scientific research team typically consists of members with different knowledge, skills, and abilities that are combined to conduct scientific experiments that none of the members could produce alone. Complementary tasks correspond to the maxim of Gestalt psychology that "the whole is greater than the sum of its parts" or the aphorism of Benjamin Franklin that "the good men may do separately is small compared with what they may do collectively" (Isaacson 2003).

Divisible and Unitary

Steiner (1972) subsequently published an influential book titled *Group Process and Productivity* that added other considerations. *Divisible* group tasks can be divided into subtasks and assigned to group members, whereas *unitary* group tasks cannot meaningfully or efficiently be divided into subtasks and assigned to different group members. For example, two people can each type different parts of a manuscript at the same time on different terminals, but they cannot efficiently type one manuscript on the same keyboard of one terminal (say, by each person typing every other letter).

Maximizing and Optimizing

Steiner (1972) further distinguished maximizing and optimizing group tasks. *Maximizing* tasks have physical criteria such as quantity, distance, or time. For example, the criterion of performance in pushing a stalled car to the edge of the highway is moving the car as fast as possible. The criterion of performance in a 400-meter relay is time. In general, there are objective criteria for maximizing tasks and typically little argument within the accuracy of measurement. In brainstorming tasks the objective is to produce as many ideas as possible rather than to produce good ideas (Diehl and Strobe 1987, 1991). *Optimizing* tasks do not have objective criteria of performance but instead are judgments of the quality of performance. For example, the criterion of success in mixed-pairs figure skating is technical performance and artistic impression rather than the physical criteria of speed or the lifted partner's weight. The criteria of performance for a college term paper are not total words but comprehensiveness, accuracy, persuasive organization, creativity, and so forth. The criterion of performance for a string quartet is not to play as fast or slow, loud or soft, as possible, but to meet standards of quality, coordination, and musicality. In general, optimizing tasks require subjective judgments of raters, evaluators, or judges on standards of quality rather than objective measurement. Because the criterion of success on optimizing tasks is subjective judgment rather than objective physical measurement, the raters, evaluators, or judges may disagree in their evaluations.

Intellective and Judgmental

Laughlin (1980) proposed a group task continuum anchored by intellective and judgmental tasks. Intellective tasks have a demonstrably correct solution within a mathematical, logical, scientific, or verbal conceptual system. For example, high school geometry problems have a definite correct solution within the axioms, postulates, definitions, and proofs of Euclidean geometry. A correct answer or proof can be demonstrated to anyone who accepts Euclidean geometry and can understand the proof. Most college physics, chemistry, and biology problems have a definite correct solution within the respective scientific systems. English vocabulary problems have a definite correct answer within the system of the English language. Some questions about the political system of the United States have a definite correct answer within the Constitution, such as the minimum age of thirty-five for the U.S. President.

In contrast, *judgmental* tasks are evaluative, behavioral, or aesthetic judgments for which no generally accepted demonstrably correct answer exists. For example, attitudes are evaluative judgments that something is good or bad, appropriate or inappropriate, attractive or unattractive. A person who is against capital punishment cannot readily demonstrate that this attitude is correct to a person who favors capital punishment, and vice versa. A person who likes a Mozart concerto, Titian portrait, Dusenberg touring car, and Brie cheese cannot demonstrate that these preferences are correct to a person who likes a Beethoven concerto, Rembrandt portrait, Packard touring car, and Limburger cheese, and vice versa. In contrast to groups facing problems with a definite correct answer, many groups face judgmental rather than intellective tasks, for example, bankers deciding on a loan, juries deciding on guilt or innocence in criminal cases, or faculty hiring committees deciding on a job candidate.

Laughlin and Ellis (1986) subsequently proposed that demonstrably correct solutions require four conditions. First, the group members must agree on a mathematical, scientific, logical, or verbal conceptual system. Second, there must be sufficient information to solve the problem. For example, there is sufficient information for a unique solution for x in a simple linear algebraic equation with one unknown such as "$x + 3 = 13$" but insufficient information for a unique solution for x and y in an equation with two unknowns such as "$x + y = 13$." Third, the group members who do not know the correct answer must have sufficient knowledge of the system to recognize the correct answer if it is proposed by one or more group members. Fourth, the correct member or members must have sufficient ability, motivation, and time to demonstrate the correct answer to the incorrect member or members.

Summary

Group problem solving involves complementary, divisible, optimizing, intellective tasks for which a demonstrably correct answer exists within a conceptual system. The objective for the group is to achieve this correct answer, in contrast to group decision making on judgmental tasks without demonstrably correct answers where the objective for the group is to achieve consensus.

LABORATORY EXPERIMENTAL RESEARCH ON GROUP PROBLEM SOLVING

The research considered in this book is based on laboratory experimental studies. Laboratory experimental research allows random assignment of participants to manipulated experimental conditions (independent variables) and systematic measurement of the results (dependent variables). Laboratory experimental research entails the power and logic of the scientific method: formulation of hypotheses from observation and existing theory, manipulation of two or more conditions (independent variables); controlled and replicable measurement of the results (dependent variables), accepted methods of analysis; and accepted criteria for interpretation and generalization of the results.

Controlled laboratory experimental research is an abstraction from more complex phenomena, and the research considered in the following chapters has typically used relatively simple problems and readily available participants such as college students in the search for basic principles that may apply to more complex problems and other populations.

OVERVIEW OF CHAPTERS

Chapter 2 considers the historical development of social combination models, which are then assessed on different types of group tasks in many of the studies in the subsequent chapters. Chapter 3 considers research on group memory, which is important in itself and is also frequently a necessary preliminary process for further group problem solving. Chapter 4 considers group ability composition and social combination processes on world knowledge tasks. Chapter 5 considers collective induction, the cooperative search for descriptive, predictive, and explanatory generalizations, rules, and principles. Chapter 6 considers letters-to-numbers problems, an interesting class of problems that entail many insightful strategies. Chapter 7 considers group-to-individual problem-solving transfer, the effect of experience in cooperative group problem solving on subsequent individual problem solving by the group members. Chapter 8 considers social choice theory, an axiomatic and deductive approach to societal problem solving by existing or possible voting procedures. Chapter 9, the concluding chapter, proposes generalizations that emerge from theory and research on group problem solving and a brief retrospective and prospective.

Chapter Two

SOCIAL COMBINATION MODELS

SMALL GROUP RESEARCHERS have taken two different approaches to understanding social influence and group processes, the *social communication* approach and the *social combination* approach (Baron and Kerr 2003). The *social communication* approach assumes that social influence may be understood by analyzing communication between the group members: the "who says what to whom under what circumstances with what effect" of classical rhetorical theory. The *social combination* approach assumes that groups combine the group member preferences by some process to formulate a single collective group response. Different assumptions of this group process may be formalized as mathematical models, and the predictions of the models may then be competitively tested against actual group performance to assess the plausibility of the assumptions about the group process formalized in the models. We now consider the historical development of social combination models.

MARJORIE SHAW'S CLASSIC STUDY

In 1932 Marjorie Shaw published an early and influential study of group versus individual problem solving. She proposed that most previous work had been limited to studies of social facilitation, the effects of an audience of observers or other co-acting individuals (such as different students independently taking notes on a classroom lecture) on individual performance, and had not involved group interaction in "an actual problematic situation which would call for real thinking to arrive at a proper solution" (1932, p. 491).

Shaw accordingly used six problems that clearly did require "real thinking." Three were hallowed object transfer problems with a demonstrably correct solution for which the minimum number of steps could be specified. These three problems, known as the Tartaglia (named for a Renaissance Italian linguist and mathematician), the Alquin (named for an eighth-century monk and scholar), and the Tower of Hanoi (named for a fancied resemblance to a pagoda), involved the transfer of objects under specified constraints. For example, the Tartaglia or "husbands and wives" problem states:

On the A side of a river are three wives (W_1, W_2, and W_3) and their husbands (H_1, H_2, and H_3). All the men but none of the women can row. Get them across to the B side of the river by means of a boat carrying only three at one time. No man will allow his wife to be in the presence of another man unless he is also there.

The Alquin is a similar problem involving cannibals and missionaries, with the constraints that all missionaries and one particular cannibal can row, the boat holds only two people, and cannibals must not outnumber missionaries in the boat or on either shore at any time. The Tower of Hanoi or disk transfer problem requires the transfer of a stack of graduated disks (largest on bottom, smallest on top) from Area 1 to Area 3, using Area 2 as a way station, moving one disk at a time, and never placing a larger disk over a smaller disk. Two of the other three problems required rearrangements of words to complete a sentence and the rearrangement of other words to complete a sonnet, and the third required routing two school buses to pick up varying numbers of children at differing locations as efficiently as possible.

Shaw used a counterbalanced design with two sessions of three problems each, so that half of her college student participants worked as individuals in Session 1 on the three object transfer problems and as cooperative four-person groups on the other three problems in Session 2. The other half of her participants worked as cooperative four-person groups in Session 1 on the object transfer problems and as individuals in Session 2 on the other problems. Over the six problems in the two sessions only 8% of the individual solutions were correct, whereas 53% of the group solutions were correct. Shaw concluded that "groups seem assured of a much larger proportion of correct answers than individuals do," which she attributed to the interaction in the groups allowing "the rejection of incorrect suggestions and the checking of errors in the group" (p. 504). Subsequently her study was frequently cited as evidence that groups are superior to individuals in problem solving, and for the importance of group interaction and error checking in this superiority.

Shaw's experiment was followed by a number of similar studies with various group tasks over the next seven decades, and the general conclusion was that groups usually perform better than average individuals on both measures of quantity and measures of quality (Steiner maximizing and optimizing tasks) but require more time (for reviews, see Baron and Kerr 2003; Brown 2002; Davis 1969, 1992; Davis, Laughlin, and Komorita 1976; Forsyth 2010; Hackman and Morris 1975; Hastie 1986; Hill 1982; Hinsz, Tindale, and Vollrath 1997; Kelley and Thibaut 1954, 1969; Kerr, MacCoun, and Kramer 1996a, 1996b; Kerr and Tindale 2004; Laughlin 1980; Levine and Moreland 1990, 1998; Lorge et al. 1958; McGrath 1984; Moreland and Levine 1992; Parks and Sanna 1999; Stasser and Dietz-Uhler 2001; and Steiner 1972).

EXPERIMENTAL DESIGNS

Shaw's experiment with a within-subjects design and counterbalanced order may be schematized as GI versus IG, where G = group and I = individual, and GI and IG indicate two successive sets of three problems. A simple between-subjects design with random assignment to group and individual conditions may be schematized as G versus I. If there are two administrations of the same task and random assignment a mixed design may be schematized as IG versus II, where participants are randomly assigned to either the IG condition or the II condition (between subjects) and there are two administrations of the same task (within subjects). This allows assessment of the social combination processes through which groups with different member preferences formulate a collective group response. A further individual administration in an IGI versus III design assesses group-to-individual transfer, which we consider in chapter 7.

THE LORGE AND SOLOMON MODEL A

In considering Shaw's (1932) study Lorge and Solomon (1955) noted that on the three object transfer problems with demonstrable solutions, two of the five groups solved all three problems and two groups did not solve any of the three problems. None of the individuals solved more than one of the three problems. This led Lorge and Solomon to suspect that the superiority of groups was not the result of the group correcting errors, as Shaw had proposed, but simply a matter of the group members' ability: "The fact that some groups solved none and some groups solved all the problems suggests the hypothesis that the observed group superiority is due to the abilities of the members of the group rather than personal interaction" (1955, p.140). Group interaction would simply be a matter of the group recognizing and adopting a correct solution if any member of the group proposed it, not such processes as rejection of errors that Shaw emphasized. The correct answer should be immediately obvious and demonstrable once proposed, so the group should solve the problem if one or more group members could solve it. Steiner (1966, 1972) later called this assumption about the group process "truth wins."

Lorge and Solomon presented an analysis that may be illustrated as follows. Assume that in a given population of individuals a proportion, P_I, can successfully solve a given problem, and a proportion, $(1 - P_I)$, cannot solve the problem. For example, 60% of a population of college students might be able to solve the Tartaglia, and 40% might be unable to solve it. The probability that a randomly sampled individual from this population will be able to solve the problem is $P_I = .60$, and the probability that the randomly sampled individual will not be able to solve the problem is $1 - P_I = .40$. Assume that groups of two persons are randomly chosen from this population. There are four types of groups—Type One: Person A can solve and Person B can solve, which occurs with probability (.60) (.60) = .36; Type Two: Person A can solve and Person B cannot solve, which occurs with probability (.60) (.40) = .24; Type Three: Person A cannot solve and Person B can solve, which occurs with probability (.40) (.60) = .24; Type Four: Person A cannot solve and Person B cannot solve, which occurs with probability (.40) (.40) = .16. Clearly Type One groups should be able to solve the problem, and Type Four groups should not be able to solve the problem. On the truth-wins assumption that the group will solve the problem if either member can solve the problem, Type Two and Type Three groups should solve the problem, so the total predicted probability that the groups will solve the problem is .36 + .24 + .24 = .84, or 84% of the groups in an experiment should solve the problem.

Lorge and Solomon then presented their famous Model A:

$$P_G = 1 - (1 - P_I)^N$$
P_G = probability a group of size N will solve the problem
P_I = probability an individual will solve the problem
N = group size

The model assumes that any group with at least one correct member will solve the problem, or all cases except when no member can solve the problem, which occurs with probability $(1 - P_I)^N$. With a probability of .60 that individuals can solve the problem the Model A predicts that groups of two, three, four, and five members will solve the problem with respective probabilities of .84, .94, .97, and .99. Lorge and Solomon tested this Model A against Shaw's data, and it fit quite well for the Tartaglia and Tower of Hanoi problems but not as well for the Alquin problem. They therefore proposed a second "Model B," which assumed that the problem consisted of two successive stages and that the group would solve the problem if any member could solve either stage. This model improved the fit for the Alquin problem.

This reconceptualization and reanalysis of Shaw's study was an impressive demonstration of Lorge and Solomon's hypothesis "that the observed group superiority is due to the abilities of the members of the group rather than personal interaction" (p. 140). However, it is important to realize that they did not strictly deny the importance of "personal interaction"; instead, they assumed that this personal interaction or group process was simply a matter of recognizing a correct answer once at least one group member proposed it and adopting it as the group response, rather than the process of correction of errors and rejection of incorrect answers that Shaw emphasized. There was a group process but not the one proposed by Shaw.

THE LORGE AND SOLOMON MODEL A AS AN APPLICATION OF THE BINOMIAL THEOREM

The Lorge-Solomon Model A is an application of the binomial theorem in probability theory. To simplify the notation, define the probability that individuals can solve the problem as p, and the probability that individuals cannot solve the problem as q. Denote group size as N. The binomial theorem gives the expansion of $(p + q)^N$. The number of possible combinations of N persons partitioned or divided into a subgroup of size $r_1 =$ solvers and a subgroup of size $r_2 =$ nonsolvers is given by $_NC_{r_1,r_2} = N! / r_1!$ $r_2!$. Assume a four-person group, a subgroup of solvers r_1 and a subgroup of nonsolvers r_2. There are five types of groups: (1) $r_1 = 4$ and $r_2 = 0$; (2) $r_1 = 3$ and $r_2 = 1$; (3) $r_1 = 2$ and $r_2 = 2$; (4) $r_1 = 1$ and $r_2 = 3$; and (5) $r_1 = 0$ and $r_2 = 4$. The numbers of combinations of the five types of groups are 1, 4, 6, 4, and 1, respectively. These are the coefficients of the binomial expansion. Keeping $p = .6$ and $q = .4$, the binomial expansion of $(p + q)^N$ is:

$$(p + q)^4 = p^4 + (4)\, p^3 q + (6)\, p^2 q^2 + (4)\, p\, q^3 + q^4.$$
$$(.6 + .4)^4 = .6^4 + (4)\, .6^3 .4 + (6)\, .6^2 .4^2 + (4)\, .6\, .4^3 + .4^4$$
$$(.6 + .4)^4 = .1296 + .3456 + .3456 + .1536 + .0256.$$

With group size $N = 4$ and $P_1 = .6$, the Lorge and Solomon Model is $P_G = 1 - (1 - P_1)^N = .9744$. Alternatively, the probability that the group will solve the problem is the sum of $.1296 + .3456 + .3456 + .1536 = .9744$.

Thus Lorge and Solomon used the binomial theorem and a truth-wins assumption of the group process to predict the probability of successful group solution. The binomial theorem could equally well be used to predict the probability of successful group solution from other assumptions of the group process. For example, a truth-supported wins assumption would be that at least two correct members are necessary for a correct group response, so that the predicted probability of a correct group response would be $.1296 + .3456 + .3456 = .8208$.

SMOKE AND ZAJONC: GROUP DECISION SCHEMES

Smoke and Zajonc (1962) introduced the concept of a group decision scheme. Like Lorge and Solomon they assumed a task with two alternatives, a known probability p of individuals being correct, and a known group size N. Then:

> If p is the probability that a given individual member is correct, the group response has a probability $h(p)$ of being correct, where $h(p)$ is a function of p depending upon the type of decision scheme accepted by the group. We shall call $h(p)$ a decision function. Intuitively, it would seem that a group decision scheme is desirable to the extent that its $h(p)$ surpasses p. (Smoke and Zajonc 1962, 322)

Thus a group decision scheme is a rule or procedure that the group uses to formulate a group decision from a number of individual decisions. Depending upon the group decision scheme that the group adopts the group will have a probability $h(p)$ of being correct. Note that $h(p)$ is a general term for any group decision scheme, whereas the corresponding P_G of Lorge and Solomon was based on only one group decision scheme, truth wins.

Smoke and Zajonc proposed four group decision schemes that specify or sum various terms of the binomial expansion. The *minimal quorum* group decision scheme assumes that the group response will be correct if any individual group member's response is correct. The decision function, $h(p)$, or probability of a correct group response, is $1 - (1 - p)^N$, where p is the probability of a correct individual response and N is the number of group members or group size. This is the Lorge and Solomon Model A, where the notation $h(p)$ corresponds to P_G and p corresponds to P_I. The *unanimity* group decision scheme assumes that the group response will be correct only if all individual responses are correct, and the decision function $h(p)$ is p^N, the first term of the binomial expansion of $(p + q)^N$. In other words, rather than assuming that the group will be correct if any one member is correct, another plausible assumption is that the group will be correct only if every member is correct. The minimal quorum and unanimity group decision schemes therefore correspond to the end points of the conjunctive-disjunctive continuum. The *fixed* group decision scheme assumes that the group response will be correct if a subgroup of fewer than all members (unanimity) but more than one member (minimum quorum) is correct. For example, it might be assumed that exactly three members of a five-person group solving a difficult problem would be necessary for the group to be correct, since two or fewer correct members would not be able to demonstrate the correct solution, and four or five correct members might try to generate a novel creative (but incorrect) answer. The *quorum* group decision scheme assumes that at least two, three, four, ..., N members must be correct for the group to be correct, and consequently sums over the corresponding terms of the binomial expansion. For example, the predicted probability $h(p)$ of a correct group response for a quorum of three correct members in four-person groups would sum over the $r_1 = 4$ and $r_2 = 0$, and $r_1 = 3$ and $r_2 = 1$, terms of the binomial expansion of $(p + q)^4$.

Because they are based on the binomial expansion, all four of these group decision schemes assume that all the members of the group have the same probability of being correct (.60 in our example) and that all the possible combinations of members in a given type of group are equivalent to one another. For example, in a four-person group of members A, B, C, and D, there are four ways in which three members may be correct and one member incorrect: Members A, B, and C are correct and Member D is incorrect; Members A, B, and D are correct and Member C is incorrect; Members A, C, and D are correct and Member B is incorrect; Members B, C, and D are correct and Member A is incorrect. In contrast, the *dictatorship* group decision scheme assumes that the group members have different probabilities of being correct and that the group response is completely determined by one particular group member, so that the group will be correct with the probability that this one particular group member, the dictator, is correct. The *oligarchy* group decision scheme assumes that the group response is completely determined by a specific subgroup of k members, where k is more than one group member (dictator) and less than N group members (unanimity). For example, Members B and D may be an oligarchy, so that the group is correct only if both Member B and Member D are correct. The subgroups of correct members are not considered equivalent to one another, as in the fixed group decision scheme. Consequently the decision function $h(p)$, or probability that the group will be correct, is p^k.

Smoke and Zajonc computed the probability of a correct group for different group decision schemes for five-person groups and values of p (individual probability of being correct) from 0 to 1.00. The most effective decision schemes are a minimal quorum, where the correct response of any single member enables the group to be correct, and a quorum of size two, where two or more correct individuals enable the group to be correct. As noted previously, Steiner (1966, 1972) later called the minimal quorum decision scheme "truth wins," and Laughlin (1980) later called the quorum of size two "truth-supported wins." Dictatorship is less effective than a minimal quorum and a quorum of size two, since the dictator must be correct for the group to be correct. Oligarchy is even less effective, since the joint probability that two or more specific individuals will be correct is less than the probability that any one of them alone will be correct.

This article of Smoke and Zajonc was of seminal importance in the development of contemporary theories of group problem solving and decision making. Lorge and Solomon had used the binomial theorem to predict group performance from the known probability of individuals being correct and the truth-wins assumption that a single correct member was necessary and sufficient for a correct group response. In introducing the concept of a group decision scheme, Smoke and Zajonc used the binomial theorem to formalize other assumptions about the group process in the quorum, fixed, and unanimity decision schemes. While the binomial expansion assumes a constant probability of being correct and incorrect for all group members, so that subgroups of a given composition of correct and incorrect members are equivalent to each other, Smoke and Zajonc also extended the analysis to group members of differing probabilities of being correct in the dictatorship and oligarchy group decision schemes.

THOMAS AND FINK: EXTENSION TO MORE THAN TWO RESPONSE ALTERNATIVES

The theorists to this point considered group tasks with only two alternatives, correct and incorrect, and used the binomial expansion of $(p + q)^N$ to form models of group performance under various assumptions of the group process. The binomial theorem is a special case of the multinomial expansion with three or more alternatives: $(p_1 + p_2 + p_3 + \ldots)^N$. Thomas and Fink (1961) extended the binomial model with two responses to a multinomial model with four responses. They proposed and tested three assumptions about the group process on the Maier and Solem (1952) Horse Trading Problem, which states: "A man bought a horse for $60 and then sold it for $70. Then he bought it back for $80 and sold it for $90. How much money did he make in the horse business?"

Thomas and Fink administered the Horse Trading Problem to individual college students and then composed cooperative groups of sizes two, three, four, or five to retake the problem. Rather than considering the responses as correct ($20.00) and incorrect, Thomas and Fink distinguished three different incorrect responses, $30.00, $10.00, and $0.00. There were four different types of groups: (1) all members were correct as individuals; (2) some members were correct and some were incorrect; (3) all members had different incorrect answers; and (4) all members had the same incorrect answer. Three different models were tested in each of the four types of groups. The *independence* model assumes that the distribution of answers for groups will not differ from the distribution of answers for individuals working alone. In other words, the independence model assumes that group interaction has no effect and that the group behaves as the members would alone. The *rational* model assumes that the group will be correct if any member of the group proposes the correct answer. This is the Lorge and Solomon Model A and the Smoke and Zajonc minimal quorum group decision scheme. The *consensus* model assumes that pressures for uniformity will increase the number of both unanimously correct and unanimously incorrect groups, so that the expected probability of a correct group answer is greater than the prediction of the independence model but less than the prediction of the rational model. Thomas and Fink tested the models from the individual probabilities of the correct and three types of incorrect responses. In general, the predictions of this consensus model fit the obtained distribution of group responses better than the predictions of the independence and consensus models.

This article made a number of important contributions to the evolving social combination approach to group problem solving and decision making. First, Thomas and Fink extended previous applications of the binomial theorem to a task with two alternatives to the more general case of the multinomial theorem, which is applicable to tasks with more than two response alternatives and of which the binomial theorem is a special case. Second, their consensus model related models of group problem solving to research on conformity, where strong pressures from unanimously incorrect members have been demonstrated against a single correct member (Allen 1965; Asch 1956). Third, they compared the predictions of their three models by conducting an experiment to test the predictions of the models for actual group performance.

DAVIS: SOCIAL DECISION SCHEME THEORY

The *social decision scheme theory* of Davis (1973) integrated and generalized the previous ideas of (a) using a known individual probability distribution for preferences of alternatives and the binomial or multinomial expansion to predict the probability of occurrence of different types of groups; and (b) formalizing assumptions about the group process as group decision schemes to predict the probability of group responses.

The theory posits a number n of mutually exclusive and exhaustive response alternatives $A_1, A_2, \ldots, A_n$, such as Correct or Incorrect on a problem, Candidates Brown, Jones, or Smith in an election, or First Degree Murder, Second Degree Murder, Manslaughter, or Not Guilty in a murder trial (note that Davis uses n for the number of alternatives, not the number of group members or group size as for the previous theorists and examples). Davis uses r for group size. In a given population of individuals there will be a probability distribution, $(p_1, p_2, \ldots, p_n)$, of preference for the alternatives. For example, we have previously used the distribution (.6, .4) for a population in which 60% of the individuals are able to solve a problem, and 40% are not able to solve the problem in our presentation of the Lorge and Solomon Model A.

Next, assume that a large number of groups of r members are assembled at random from this population (r = group size). For a given group size r there will be a number of different possible types of groups or combinations of individual preferences for the alternatives. The number of combinations (C) or distinguishable distributions of member preferences (types of groups) is given by Equation 2.1

$$m = {}_{(n + r - 1)}C_r \qquad \text{Equation 2.1}$$

where n = number of alternatives, r = group size.

For example, for $n = 2$ and $r = 4$, $m = {}_{(2 + 4 - 1)}C_4 = 5! / 4! \ 1! = 5$. We have previously considered the five types of four-person groups with two alternatives correct and incorrect, which we may denote as $(4 - 0)$, $(3 - 1)$, $(2 - 2)$, $(1 - 3)$, $(0 - 4)$.

Given the probability distribution of individual preferences for the response alternatives, the probability π of each of these m distinguishable distributions of member preferences is given by the multinomial expansion of $(p_1 + p_2 + \ldots + p_n)^r$

The π values may then be arranged as a π row vector.

Davis then introduces the concept of a social decision scheme, D, which corresponds to Smoke and Zajonc's (1962) group decision scheme. A social decision scheme is a rule or procedure by which the group combines a distribution of member preferences in a collective group response. This rule or procedure may be prescribed by the constitution or bylaws of the group, by law, by tradition, or may be assumed by a theory. For example, Robert's Rules of Order prescribe a simple majority voting rule for most committees and parliamentary procedures.

Formally a social decision scheme is an $m \times n$ matrix $D_h = [d_{ij}]$, in which each element of the matrix is the probability that the group will select the jth alternative given the ith distribution of member preferences. For example, the Smoke and Zajonc minimal quorum group decision scheme (truth wins) with four-person groups and the response alternatives correct and incorrect is formalized by the 5×2 matrix $D_{truth\ wins}$, as given in Table 2.1.

TABLE 2.1
Social Decision Scheme Matrix for a Truth-Wins Social Combination Process

Distribution of Members		Probability of Group Response	
Correct	Incorrect	Correct	Incorrect
4	0	1.00	.00
3	1	1.00	.00
2	2	1.00	.00
1	3	1.00	.00
0	4	.00	1.00

TABLE 2.2
Social Decision Scheme Matrix for a Truth-Supported-Wins
Social Combination Process

Distribution of Members		Probability of Group Response	
Correct	Incorrect	Correct	Incorrect
4	0	1.00	.00
3	1	1.00	.00
2	2	1.00	.00
1	3	.00	1.00
0	4	.00	1.00

The social decision scheme matrix $D_{truth\text{-}supported\,wins}$ (Smoke and Zajonc's quorum size two group decision scheme), where two correct members are necessary and sufficient for a correct group response is given in Table 2.2.

A majority social decision scheme assumes that the group response is the response that a majority of group members favor. If there is no majority, an equiprobability subscheme assumes that each response is equally likely, as when the chair votes to break a tie under Roberts' Rules of Order or the vice president votes to break a tie in the U.S. Senate. The matrix $D_{majority}$ is given in Table 2.3.

The predicted distribution of group responses $(P_1, P_2, \ldots, P_n)$ is then computed by postmultiplying the π row vector by the social decision scheme matrix D, as given in Equation 2.2. Note that upper case P is used for the distribution of group responses and lower case p is used for the distribution of individual responses.

$$(P_1, P_2, \ldots, P_n) = (\neq_1, \neq_2, \ldots, \neq_m) \begin{pmatrix} d_{11}, d_{12}, \ldots d_{1n} \\ d_{21}, d_{22}, \ldots d_{2n} \\ \cdots \\ d_{m1}, d_{m2}, \ldots d_{mn} \end{pmatrix}$$ Equation 2.2

For our example of the two response alternatives Correct = C and Incorrect = I, four-person groups, individual probability distribution (.60, .40) and $D_{truth\,wins}$:

$$(P_C, P_I) = (.1296, .3456, .3456, .1536, .0256) \begin{pmatrix} 1.00, & .00 \\ 1.00, & .00 \\ 1.00, & .00 \\ 1.00, & .00 \\ .00 & 1.00 \end{pmatrix}$$

$$(P_C, P_I) = (.9744, .0256)$$

TABLE 2.3
Social Decision Scheme Matrix for a Majority Social Combination Process

Distribution of Members		Probability of Group Response	
Correct	Incorrect	Correct	Incorrect
4	0	1.00	.00
3	1	1.00	.00
2	2	.50	.50
1	3	.00	1.00
0	4	.00	1.00

This is the same result as the Lorge and Solomon Model A and the Smoke and Zajonc minimal quorum group decision scheme. The $D_{truth\text{-}supported\ wins}$ social decision scheme predicts $(P_C, P_I) = (.8208, .1792)$, and the $D_{majority}$ social decision scheme predicts $(P_C, P_I) = (.6480, .3520)$.

The predictions of these and any other desired social decision schemes may then be tested in an experiment with a sufficient number of groups for statistical power by standard goodness of fit statistics (e.g., Chi-square or Kolmogorov-Smirnov).

With more than two alternatives the procedures are the same, although computationally more complex. To illustrate, assume four-person groups and the three alternatives A, B, and C. Equation 2.1 indicates that there are fifteen possible distributions of member preferences. The probabilities of these fifteen distributions are computed from the general term of the multinomial expansion.

Finally, as two row vectors and a matrix, Equation 2.2 may be expressed in unsubscripted form as Equation 2.3:

$$P = \pi D \qquad\qquad \text{Equation 2.3}$$

MODEL TESTING AND MODEL FITTING

Kerr, Stasser, and Davis (1979) distinguish model testing and model fitting to assess the relationships between social combination models and group performance. In *model testing* the probabilities of individual responses are used to test each of a number of a priori models of interest such as majority, proportionality, or truth wins against the matrix of group responses (columns) for member preference distributions (rows) to determine whether the predictions of each model may be rejected. Models that are not rejected are then plausible (but not necessary) explanations of the underlying group processes in mapping a distribution of member preferences to a collective group response.

In *model fitting* the researcher examines the matrix of group responses for member preference distributions for orderly processes such as majority, proportionality, or truth wins. This may provide a plausible a posteriori explanation of the group processes. This plausible a posteriori model from model fitting may then be tested as an a priori model in a further experiment. In chapter 5 we consider an example of this procedure of model fitting to formulate a plausible a posteriori model by inspection in one experiment followed by a priori testing of the model in a new experiment.

If research participants first respond as individuals and then respond again as a cooperative group, the composition of each group (for example, five correct and none incorrect, four correct and one incorrect, etc.) is known. This gives an obtained matrix of group responses for each member distribution. The predictions of different social combination models (social decision schemes) may then be tested against this obtained matrix. Kerr et al. (1976) called this another type of model fitting.

Summary

Shaw (1932) compared groups and individuals on intellective problems, and concluded that groups performed better than individuals because the group members recognized and corrected erroneous responses. Lorge and Solomon (1955) used the binomial theorem and the truth-wins assumption that the group would recognize and adopt a correct solution if proposed by at least one group member to predict the probability of a correct group solution from the known probability of individual solutions. Smoke and Zajonc (1962) introduced the concept of group decision schemes and formalized a number of other assumptions about the group process, such as quorums of various sizes or oligarchy. Thomas and Fink (1961) extended the approach to tasks with more than two alternatives, using the individual probabilities of correct and three different incorrect responses to test their models. Davis (1973), in his theory of social decision schemes, integrated and generalized the application of the multinomial theorem and the concept of group decision schemes in an elegant matrix algebra formulation. A social decision scheme formalizes any assumption about the group process that assigns probabilities of each group response given each distribution of member preferences. The assumptions may come from the constitutions or bylaws of a group, from previous research, or any other hypothesized group process. Different social decision schemes or social combination models may then be tested competitively against actual group performance as a test of the assumptions formalized by the social decision schemes. Stasser (1999) gives an excellent overall presentation of social decision scheme theory, including model formation, model testing, and using the equations for prospective modeling. Different a priori social decision schemes or social combination models may be tested against the matrix of obtained group responses for member preference distributions (model testing), or the matrix may be examined to induce a plausible a posteriori model (model fitting). In the following chapters we consider social decision schemes, or social combination models, on different group tasks.

Chapter Three

MEMORY AND GROUP PROBLEM SOLVING

IN THE PROCESS of problem solving, both individuals and groups process information to formulate, evaluate, and select alternatives that change a current less desirable state to a more desirable future state. After some of this information is presented in the given problem state, further information must be retrieved from the memories of the group members. Thus a basic process in group problem solving is group memory for information. Just as individual memory involves processes of encoding, storage, and retrieval of information, group memory involves the same three interpersonal processes (Hinsz, Tindale, and Vollrath 1997). Individual memory may require recognition of correct alternatives among a set of possibilities, such as multiple-choice or true-false examinations, or recall of correct information, as in "fill in the blanks" or essay examinations. Similarly, group memory may require recognition of correct alternatives among set of possibilities or recall of information. Research on group recognition memory has typically considered such memory an end in itself. Research on group recall memory has emphasized the distribution of information among the group members. The information may be knowledge possessed by the group members prior to an experiment, just as they bring their personality traits and attributes, or it may be information assigned to the different group members to learn prior to subsequent group problem solving.

Accordingly, we first consider group memory based on knowledge possessed by the group members prior to an experiment. The major emphasis in this research for the past quarter-century has been *transactive memory,* a shared system for encoding, storing, and retrieving information (Wegner 1986). We then consider group problem solving based on memory for information assigned to the different group members to learn prior to subsequent group problem solving. The major emphasis in this area is *shared and unshared information* beginning with a landmark study of Stasser and Titus (1985). We then consider an extensive study of jury memory, which is based on both information possessed by the group members prior to the trial and information presented during the trial prior to jury deliberation.

RECOGNITION MEMORY

Earlier research on group versus individual recognition memory has been thoroughly reviewed by Clark and Stevenson (1989) and Hartwick, Sheppard, and Davis (1982). These reviews clearly indicate that group recognition memory is superior to the memory of the average individual. In a more recent experiment by Hinsz (1990) college students watched a videotape of a simulated job interview of an applicant for a position as a management trainee in a record store chain. The students then answered true-false questions about the interview, for example, "The job applicant began his work experience in 1978." They also indicated their confidence in their answers for each question. Their response sheets were collected, and then they answered the same questions again as cooperative six-person groups or as individuals.

The individual and group responses were analyzed by signal detection theory. Signal detection theory assumes a true state and a response for each item. The true state of the interview was that the information was either presented or not presented, and the response was that the information was either presented or not presented, as given in Table 3.1.

The groups had significantly better memory performance than the individuals on the second administration of the items for each of (a) proportion of correct responses (hits plus correct rejections); (b) proportion of hits; (c) proportion of correct rejections; and (d) d', the z score for hits minus the z score for false alarms. As warranted by their superior performance, the groups were more confident in their answers than the individuals.

Table 3.2 gives six possible social decision schemes. The decision schemes give the predicted probabilities of correct and incorrect group responses for each of the seven possible distributions of group members, six correct and none incorrect (6-0), five correct and one incorrect (5-1), . . . , none correct and six incorrect (0-6). Truth wins predicts a correct group response if at least one group member is correct, Truth-supported wins if at least two group members are correct, Plurality if at

TABLE 3.1
Signal Detection Theory Matrix

	True State	
Response	Presented	Not Presented
Presented	hit	false alarm
Not Presented	miss	correct rejection

TABLE 3.2
Six Possible Social Decision Schemes

Distribution	Truth Wins		Truth Supp		Plurality		4–6 Major		5–6 Major		Unan	
	Cor	Inc	Cor	Inc	Cor	Inc	Cor	Inc	Cor	Inc	Cor	Inc
6–0	1.00	.00	1.00	.00	1.00	.00	1.00	.00	1.00	.00	1.00	.00
5–1	1.00	.00	1.00	.00	1.00	.00	1.00	.00	1.00	.00	.00	1.00
4–2	1.00	.00	1.00	.00	1.00	.00	1.00	.00	.00	1.00	.00	1.00
3–3	1.00	.00	1.00	.00	1.00	.00	.00	1.00	.00	1.00	.00	1.00
2–4	1.00	.00	1.00	.00	.00	1.00	.00	1.00	.00	1.00	.00	1.00
1–5	1.00	.00	.00	1.00	.00	1.00	.00	1.00	.00	1.00	.00	1.00
0–6	.00	1.00	.00	1.00	.00	1.00	.00	1.00	.00	1.00	.00	1.00

Note: Truth Supp = Truth-supported wins; 4–6 Major = 4–6 Majority; 5–6 Major = 5–6 Majority; Unan = Unanimity; Cor = Correct; Inc = Incorrect.

least three group members are correct, 4/6 Majority if at least four group members are correct, 5/6 Majority if at least five group members are correct, and Unanimity only if all six group members are correct.

Table 3.3 gives the observed social decision scheme for the group recognition responses across all groups and items. As indicated in Table 3.3 the groups were very likely to be correct if at least four members were correct, and had a probability of .77 of being correct when three members were correct. The predictions of the six models were tested against the observed data, and the best-fitting model was Plurality with at least three correct members (this is an unusual use of plurality, which typically assumes three or more alternatives, as in the theory and research

TABLE 3.3
Observed Social Decision Scheme for
Group Responses over All Items

Member		Group	
Correct	Incorrect	Correct	Incorrect
6	0	.98	.02
5	1	.94	.06
4	2	.88	.12
3	3	.77	.23
2	4	.61	.39
1	5	.41	.59
0	6	.33	.67

Source: Hinsz 1990.

TABLE 3.4
Probability Group Correct for Low, Medium,
and High Member Confidence

Members		Member Confidence		
Cor	Inc	Low	Med	High
6	0	.93	.97	1.00
5	1	.89	.94	.96
4	2	.80	.91	.94
3	3	.67	.82	.86
2	4	.54	.63	.74
1	5	.34	.46	.59
0	6	.42	.09	.33

Source: Hinsz 1990.

we consider in chapter 8 on social choice theory). Note also that Hinsz knew whether the group members were correct as individuals on the first administration of the recognition test and thus knew the composition of each group, so the analysis was a type of model fitting. There was no need to estimate the probabilities of the different distributions of group members from an independent sample of individuals, as in the original procedure of Lorge and Solomon (1955) and the model-testing procedures of social decision scheme theory (Davis 1973).

Hinsz (1990) then trichotomized the items into those for which the group had high, medium, or low confidence of being correct. Table 3.4 gives the obtained probabilities of correct and incorrect group responses for high, medium, and low confidence. As indicated in Table 3.4, fewer correct group members were required for a correct group response as the confidence of the group in being correct increased.

In summary, group recognition memory was superior to individual memory for the performance measures of correct answers (hits plus correct rejections), hits, correct rejections, and d'. Three correct group members were generally sufficient for a correct group response, especially as confidence in their responses increased.

TRANSACTIVE MEMORY

Individual memory processes involve encoding information, storing the encoded information, and retrieving the stored information. Over the course of history, knowledge develops and is represented as written languages, mathematical and scientific systems, musical notation, maps and diagrams, and many other representational systems. This knowledge is stored in books, archives, data banks, constitutions, laws, computer applications and documents, among many other forms, so that we now have access to the knowledge that was discovered, created, organized, and elaborated by our predecessors. All these representational systems of knowledge may be considered *external* memory aids.

Wegner (1986) proposed that in addition to these external memory aids other *people* may also serve as external memory aids. Interacting people may have a *transactive memory system,* which Wegner defines as a shared system for encoding, storing, and retrieving information. An example is a married couple. One person may concentrate on learning and remembering information about food and beverages, shopping, and preparing meals, while the other person pays their bills, upgrades their computer, prepares their joint income tax return, and handles their investments. In this way transactive memory systems expand individual knowledge and expertise, enable specialization, and hence contribute to a better collective than individual performance.

No Communication during Learning or Retrieval

Wegner, Erber, and Raymond (1991) conducted the first experiment motivated by this explicit concept of transactive memory, in contrast to earlier work that was simply called "group memory." They recruited dating couples for an experiment on learning by cooperative pairs, reasoning that the dating couples would have developed a transactive memory system based on their shared experience and recognition of their complementary knowledge, abilities, and interests. In contrast, previously unacquainted college students who first meet each other as participants in the learning experiment would not have developed a transactive memory system. The authors reasoned that imposing a structured memory system assigning each member to learn part of the information should hinder the dating couples by disrupting their existing transactive memory system but help previously unacquainted couples by enabling them to specialize by learning different parts of the information.

The participants were pairs of college students who had dated each other for at least three months. The task was to learn underlined words on sixteen cards with four statements per card from seven categories: science, food, spelling, alcohol, history, television, and psychology. For example, a statement in the category of science was: "Yeasts reproduce by budding." Half the dating couples (called "natural pairs") were randomly assigned to learn the words with their partners, whereas the other half (called "impromptu pairs") learned the words with a stranger. All the dating pairs first rated which member was better at each category.

Half the natural pairs and half the impromptu pairs were then assigned to learn one of these sets of categories, whereas the other half of the natural and impromptu pairs were not assigned categories of words to learn. All the natural or impromptu pairs then learned the items individually, without communicating with each other. Although they expected to be tested as a pair, they were actually tested individually without communicating with each other. In summary, the experiment used a 2 × 2 between-groups factorial design, with the variables pairs (natural or impromptu) and categories to be learned (assigned or not assigned).

The previously unacquainted impromptu pairs learned more words with an imposed memory system (mean = 30.14) than without an imposed memory system (mean = 27.64), whereas the previously acquainted natural pairs learned more words without an imposed memory system (mean = 31.40) than with an imposed memory system (mean = 27.64). The authors interpreted this finding as indicating that imposing new inconsistent learning requirements on a pair with a previously developed transactive memory interfered with learning. For example, one of the pair might be a psychology major and the other a history major, so that requiring the psychology major to learn the history words and the history major to learn the psychology words would disrupt learning based on their transactive memory system. In contrast, assigning the categories to previously unacquainted pairs would not interfere with a previously developed transactive memory system and could reduce the difficulty of the learning task by enabling them to specialize in learning categories of words.

Although these results supported the authors' predictions, the experiment did not fully test the theory of transactive memory as a shared system for encoding, storing, and retrieving information. The participants learned the words separately without interacting and recalled the words separately without interacting. The scoring system gave the couples credit for the number of words recalled by each noninteracting member, and thus was an additive task for noninteracting group members rather than a complementary task for interacting group members.

Communication during Retrieval

Hollingshead (1998c) assessed communication during retrieval in transactive memory. As in Wegner, Erber, and Raymond (1991) she recruited dating couples who presumably had developed a transactive memory system. The experimental task was a Knowledge Test with four items in each of five categories: science, entertainment, sports, food, and American history. One example from the science category was the question, "What nuclear process takes place in a hydrogen bomb?" All participants first answered the Knowledge Test individually without communicating.

TABLE 3.5
Mean Correct Information Items for Individuals on First Administration,
for Dating and Stranger Couples with Face-to-face and
Computer-mediated Communication on Second Administration,
and Individuals on Third Administration

		Administration		
		First	Second	Third
Dating	Face-to-face	7.4	12.3	12.1
	Computer	7.4	9.6	10.0
Stranger	Face-to-face	7.4	9.6	9.5
	Computer	7.4	10.5	10.5

Source: Hollingshead 1998c.

Then half the couples answered the same items with their dating partner, discussing face-to-face or interacting through networked computer terminals, and the other half answered the items with a stranger of the opposite gender, likewise discussing face-to-face or interacting through networked computer terminals. All the participants then answered the same items again individually. In summary, the experimental design was IGI with a 2×2 factorial for the G administration with the variables partner (dating or stranger) and communication modality (face-to-face or computer-mediated).

Table 3.5 gives the mean number of items answered correctly by the individuals on the first administration, cooperatively by the pairs on the second administration, and individually on the third administration of the Knowledge Test. As indicated in Table 3.5, the dating couples answered more items correctly with face-to-face communication than computer-mediated communication, whereas the stranger couples answered more items correctly with computer-mediated communication than face-to-face communication.

If both members of the pair knew an item on the first administration, or if neither member knew the item on the first administration, there was no difference between the dating and stranger couples for face-to-face and computer-mediated discussion. In contrast, if only one member knew the item, the dating couples with face-to-face discussion performed better than the other three conditions, presumably because the member who did not know the item knew that the other member had expertise in the area. Analysis of the discussions showed that the stranger couples made more statements about their own expertise and asked more questions about their partner's expertise than the dating couples. This was an attempt by the stranger couples to develop an efficient division of labor, in contrast to the dating couples who already had this knowledge about their own and their partner's expertise.

In a second experiment dating couples first took the same Information Test individually and then retook the Information Test with their partner in one of three communication conditions. In Condition One they could see each other but were not allowed to talk to each other, and communicated by passing written notes. In Condition Two they were separated by a screen so that they could talk to each other but not see each other. In Condition Three they could not see or hear each other, and communicated by passing notes. The mean number of correct answers was 7.6 for individuals on the first administration, and 11.0, 11.3, and 9.0 for pairs in Conditions One, Two, and Three, respectively, indicating that the cooperative retrieval of information in transactive memory was facilitated by cues that were nonverbal (gestures, etc.) or paralinguistic (loud voice, etc.).

Communication during Learning and Retrieval

Hollingshead (1998a) assessed both the importance of communication during learning and the importance of communication during retrieval in transactive memory. Again, dating couples were recruited and then randomly assigned to work with their partner or a stranger. The task was to learn six words from each of six categories: geography, fashion, alcohol, math, grammar, and movies. There were six one-minute trials of six words, one per category, presented on cards. The instructions explained that the task was to learn the words and later be tested for their learning. In four different conditions for each of the dating and stranger couples the pairs were allowed or not allowed to communicate during learning, and allowed or not allowed to communicate during retrieval. The pairs were told that they would be scored for the number of correct words recalled by either person and words recalled by both persons would count only once. After the instructions, the participants in all conditions were given one minute to plan their strategy. In summary, the experiment used a 2 × 2 × 2 between-groups design with the variables couples (dating or stranger), communication during learning (yes or no), and communication during retrieval (yes or no).

Table 3.6 gives the mean number of words recalled by just one member of the pair (unique), both members (overlapping), and the total over unique and overlapping for dating couples or stranger couples who were allowed or not allowed to communicate during learning. As indicated in Table 3.6, the dating couples learned more than the stranger couples when they did not communicate during learning, and the stranger couples learned more than the dating couples with communication during

TABLE 3.6
Mean Words Recalled for Dating and Stranger Couples
with and without Communication during Learning

Condition	Total	Unique	Overlapping
Dating, no communication	28[a]	15[a]	13[a]
Dating, communication	27[b]	15[a]	12[a]
Stranger, no communication	27[b]	12[a]	16[a]
Stranger, communication	28[a]	21[b]	8[b]

Note: Means not sharing the same subscripts in each column differ significantly, $p < .05$.
Source: Hollingshead 1998a.

learning. The stranger couples who communicated during learning had
the most unique words and fewest overlapping words, indicating an effective division of labor.

Table 3.7 gives the mean number of words recalled by one member of
the pair (unique), both members (overlapping), and the total over unique
and overlapping for pairs who were allowed or not allowed to communicate during learning and pairs who were allowed or not allowed to communicate during retrieval (summing over dating pairs and stranger pairs).
As indicated in Table 3.7, there was more learning with the same communication condition for both learning and retrieval (communication for
both or communication for neither) than different communication conditions for learning and retrieval (communication for one but not for the
other). Communication during both learning and retrieval resulted in the
most unique and the fewest overlapping recalled words, indicating that
an efficient division of labor for learning required communication during
both learning and retrieval.

TABLE 3.7
Mean Words Recalled for Communication or
No Communication during Learning and Communication
or No Communication during Retrieval

Learning	Retrieval	Total	Unique	Overlapping
No communication	No communication	29[a]	17[b]	12[a]
No communication	Communication	26[b]	10[c]	16[a]
Communication	No communication	27[b]	14[c]	13[a]
Communication	Communication	28[a]	22[a]	7[b]

Note: Means not sharing the same subscripts in each column differ significantly, $p < .05$.
Source: Hollingshead 1998a.

In summary, the dating couples recalled more than the stranger couples when they were not able to communicate during learning, and the stranger couples recalled more than the dating couples when they were able to communicate during learning. Communication during learning disrupted the dating couple's existing transactive memory system, whereas it enabled the stranger couples to develop a transactive memory system. Learning for both dating and stranger couples was better when communication was allowed during both learning and retrieval, when they used an existing transactive memory system or developed one, or not allowed during either learning or retrieval, when they relied more on their individual rather than cooperative learning and retrieval.

Nine Propositions

Hollingshead (1998b) integrated the findings of her 1998a and 1998c studies in nine propositions. Propositions 1–4 involve comparison processes to determine what each person knows. Proposition 5 establishes expertise: Who should know? Propositions 6–8 involve searching for information. Proposition 9 involves communicating knowledge by nonverbal and paralinguistic cues.

Proposition 1. Groups begin their discussion by comparing answers or preferences.

Proposition 2. If all group members retrieve the same answer, it is likely that the group will assume that answer is accurate with little or no discussion regarding whether it actually is accurate.

Proposition 3. If group members retrieve different answers, or if only one member or a subset of group members retrieve an answer, the group will need to assess its accuracy. The group must first establish and recognize expertise.

Proposition 4. If no group members are able to retrieve the answer, the group will develop and execute a shared information search strategy. The group must establish and recognize expertise before executing that shared strategy.

Proposition 5. If relative expertise is established and the recognized expert has an answer, the group will adopt the answer. Otherwise, the group will implement an information search.

Proposition 6. When group members are unable to remember shared knowledge, they will try to cue one another by engaging in a transactive information search.

Proposition 7. If the group has not reached consensus regarding the correct answer, members will focus their attention on cueing the recognized experts in an information search.

Proposition 8. If the group agrees that the correct answer is outside the collective knowledge of all members, the group will generate a guess or will look to information sources outside the group.

Proposition 9. Nonverbal and paralinguistic cues are important in the retrieval and communication of knowledge in transactive memory systems.

Cognitive Interdependence and Convergent Expectations

Hollingshead (2001) proposed that transactive memory structures involve (a) *integration*, where two persons know or learn the same information; and (b) *differentiation*, where two persons know or learn different information. Given such integration and differentiation, she proposed that the two fundamental processes in transactive memory are (a) *cognitive interdependence*, and (b) *convergent expectations*. *Cognitive interdependence* means that each person's outcomes depend on a combination of his or her own performance and the performance of the other person. *Convergent expectations* are what each person expects about the knowledge or learning of the other person: agreement on who knows what or will learn what.

The participants first indicated their own expertise in eighteen categories: English, recent movies, fashion, sports, cooking, geography, music, math, alcoholic beverages, current events, computers, automobiles, office work, pets, campus buildings, local restaurants, academic subjects, and the library. They were then instructed that they would learn six words in each of the eighteen categories with a partner who has similar expertise or different expertise. They will be scored together but will not communicate during learning or retrieval.

There were four incentive structures or scoring systems: (a) *unique recall*: the score is the number of items recalled by one member but not the other, and items recalled by both do not count (maximum differentiation); (b) *union recall*: the score is the number of items recalled by either member, and items recalled by both count once; (c) *sum recall*: the score is the number of items recalled by either member, and items recalled by both count twice; (d) *intersection recall*: the score is the number of items recalled by both members, and items recalled by only one member do not count (maximum integration).

The instructions explained that participants would first circle their own areas of expertise on a sheet with a column listing the eighteen categories. Then they would receive a page with their own areas of expertise and their partner's areas circled. These circled areas were either similar or different depending on the condition. Then one of the four incentive structures (scoring systems) was explained. After this, the participants took a quiz to make sure they understood their own and their partner's areas of expertise and the incentive structure (scoring system).

Each participant then studied a sheet with the eighteen categories, six words per category, for four minutes. The sheet was collected and the participant received a new sheet with the eighteen categories and was asked to write the six words for each category. Afterward the participants were given a new sheet listing the eighteen categories and were told to circle the categories they learned and those they thought their partner learned.

In summary, the experiment used a 2 × 4 between-groups design with the variables partner expertise (similar or different) and incentive structure (unique, union, sum, or intersection). The participants learned the items individually without interacting with the partner with the same or different expertise.

Summing over the same and different expertise conditions, the means for the consideration of the partner's expertise (higher indicates more) for the four incentive structures (scoring systems) were 4.78 for unique, 3.79 for union, 3.14 for sum, and 4.36 for intersection. The participants considered the expertise of their partner significantly more in the unique recall condition (incentive to recall different words than the partner) and the intersection recall condition (incentive to recall the same words as the partner) than the sum recall condition (incentive to recall as many words as possible, regardless of the partner's expertise). Thus the participants considered the expertise of their partner more when their outcomes were interdependent than when their outcomes were not interdependent.

Figure 3.1 gives the mean number of words recalled with partners with different expertise (top) and partners with similar expertise (bottom). As indicated in Figure 3.1, there were three major results. First, participants in the unique and union conditions recalled more in their categories of expertise and less in categories outside their expertise when they expected their partner to have different rather than similar knowledge (differentiation leads to better outcomes). Second, participants in the intersection condition recalled more in categories of expertise and less in categories outside expertise when they expected their partner to have similar rather than different knowledge (integration leads to better outcomes). Third, there was less difference for participants in the union and sum conditions (differentiation and integration lead to equal outcomes) than in the unique and intersection incentive conditions.

Hollingshead (2001) then proposed two general conclusions. First, transactive memory structures are most differentiated when individuals have different expertise and there are incentives for each individual to remember different information, and they are most integrated when individuals have similar expertise and there are incentives to remember the same information. Second, it is not necessarily past group interaction or

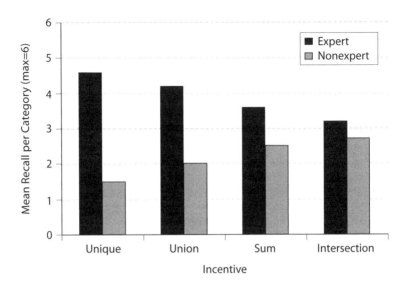

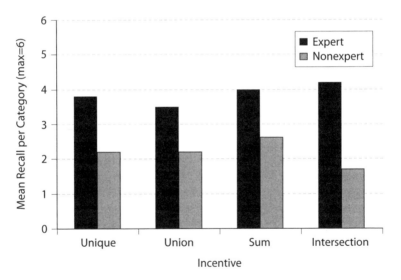

Figure 3.1. Mean Word Recall with Different (top) and Similar (bottom) Partner (Hollingshead 2001)

a close personal or working relationship, per se, that explains the development of transactive memory structures but, rather, the fundamental processes of cognitive interdependence and convergent expectations that often occur in these situations.

The construct of cognitive interdependence adds a motivational process to the cognitive processes expressed in the nine propositions of Hollingshead's (1998b) earlier theory: people prefer the better outcomes that result from coordination with another person to the poorer outcomes that result from lack of coordination with another person. The construct of convergent expectations is a superordinate category that includes the cognitive processes specified in Hollingshead's (1998b) first eight propositions. Close personal or working relationships are not the cause of transactive memory systems but the settings in which transactive memory systems develop through the two basic processes of cognitive interdependence (the members must coordinate their learning to achieve good outcomes) and convergent expectations (the members must know what each member is going to do to achieve good outcomes). The two conclusions extend the theory of transactive memory to a theory of transactive learning.

Shared and Unshared Information

Optimal Assignment of Items to Members

Zajonc and Smoke (1959) proposed a theoretical analysis of the optimal assignment of items to be learned by the different group members to maximize subsequent group recall for the items. They used a model of group memory based on three assumptions:

(a) The probability $p(i,j)$ that item i is remembered by individual j is equal to the constant p, $0 < p < 1.0$, or to zero according to whether item i is assigned to individual j;

(b) Each individual is assigned the same number, h, of items. Thus, $\Sigma i \, p(i,j) = hp$; and

(c) Each item is assigned to an equal number, n, of individuals. Thus the probability P, that a given item is recalled by at least one group member (and thus the group) is given by $P = 1 - (1 - p)^n$, the same for all items (Zajonc and Smoke 1959, p. 362).

Zajonc and Smoke (1959) then derived an individual memory model from Woodworth's (1938) empirical data. This model specifies the relationship between p and h as $p = \exp [-k^2h^2]$, where k is an empirical constant that is dependent on the difficulty of the material (items) to be remembered. Zajonc and Smoke then assumed that the number of items can be conceptualized as a continuous variable of the amount of information, and demonstrated that P, n, and h are differentiable functions of p. They then obtained the optimal values of P, n, and h by setting the appropriate partial derivatives at zero (for details, see Zajonc and Smoke 1959). This led to the surprising conclusion that, regardless of group size, group memory is maximized by assigning each member (individual) 16% more items than they can recall, or $p = .84$.

Tindale and Sheffey (2002) conducted an experimental test of the Zajonc and Smoke (1959) theoretical analysis. Sets of five college students first studied a list of CVC (consonant vowel consonant) trigrams, such as DOL, LIV, or KAN (taken from Archer 1960) for five minutes and then were given ten minutes to write as many trigrams as they could recall on a response sheet. In the Totally Shared condition each of the five persons learned the same list of forty-seven CVC trigrams. In the Partially Shared condition each of the five persons learned a different list of nineteen CVC trigrams. These five lists were set up so that the forty-seven items were presented across the five persons, and two persons received each item. The five persons then recalled the items together as a group.

Consistent with the Zajonc and Smoke (1959) analysis, the Partially Shared groups (mean = 42.21) recalled significantly more items than the Totally Shared groups (mean = 37.70). Thus distributing the items so that each member learned two rather than all items resulted in better group memory. There was less inter-item interference in learning nineteen items than all forty-seven items, and the groups were able to combine the items learned by the different members in a common group recall memory.

Table 3.8 gives the observed social decision scheme for the Totally Shared groups. As indicated in Table 3.8, there was a very high probability of a correct group recall when at least two members recalled the

TABLE 3.8
Observed Social Decision Scheme for Group Responses
for Totally Shared Information

Member		Group	
Recalled	Not Recalled	Recalled	Not Recalled
5	0	.96	.04
4	1	.98	.02
3	2	.95	.05
2	3	.91	.09
1	4	.75	.25
0	5	.26	.74

Source: Tindale and Sheffey 2002.

item (truth-supported wins) and a reasonably high probability of .75 of a correct group recall when only one member recalled the item.

In summary, the better group recall memory for the Partially Shared condition than the Totally Shared condition supports the Zajonc and Smoke (1959) model, and there was a strong truth-supported wins social combination process for the Totally Shared condition.

SHARED AND UNSHARED KNOWLEDGE

Information Sampling Model

In an extremely influential article Stasser and Titus (1985) proposed the Information Sampling Model:

$$p(D) = 1 - [1 - p(M)]_n$$
$p(D)$ = probability group discusses item
$p(M)$ = probability group member mentions item
n = group size

This model is formally equivalent to the Lorge and Solomon (1955) model and predicts that the probability a group will discuss an item increases with group size n. Stasser and Titus gave four persons information to be learned about three candidates for Student Body President before making a group choice of the best candidate. They distributed favorable and unfavorable information about the three candidates across the four members in two ways. In the Shared Information condition, all four members received information that favored the optimal candidate. In the Unshared Information condition, all four members received information that favored a suboptimal candidate, and different items that favored the optimal candidate were distributed over the different group members. Thus, if the group members mentioned their unique distributed information that favored the optimal candidate and the group discussed and integrated it, the group would make an optimal decision. However, if the group members did not mention the distributed information but only discussed the common information that favored the suboptimal candidate, the group would make a suboptimal decision.

The results were striking. In the Shared Information condition 83% of the groups chose the optimal candidate, but in the Unshared Information condition only 16% of the groups chose the optimal candidate. The groups in the Unshared Information condition discussed only the common information and did not discuss and integrate the unique information known only by one member. Stasser and Titus (1987) replicated this finding under four different conditions of twelve or twenty-four items of information and one-third or two-third of shared information. This *hidden profile effect* is extremely robust and has been replicated in many experiments (for representative reviews, see Stasser 1992; Stasser and Titus 2003; Stasser, Vaughn, and Stewart 2000).

Solving a Problem versus Making a Judgment

In this tradition of research on shared and unshared member information the experiment that is most relevant to group problem solving was conducted by Stasser and Stewart (1992). Participants learned either shared or unshared (profile) information that implicated one of three suspects in a murder case before making a group decision in three-person or six-person groups about the guilty suspect. Following the distinction between intellective tasks with demonstrably correct solutions and judgmental tasks without demonstrably correct solutions (see chapter 1) Stasser and Stewart compared "solve" and "judge" sets. In the solve set the instructions were that "only one of the suspects could have committed the crime. We would like you to read over the materials carefully and decide who you think committed the crime." In the judge set the instructions were that "the detectives in the case do not have sufficient information in the case to charge anybody for the homicide . . . we are asking you to use the available evidence and decide which of the suspects seems most likely to have committed the crime" (1992, p. 429). Stasser and Stewart reasoned that the participants with the solve set would be more likely to present and consider the information possessed by only one member, discuss it more thoroughly, and hence be more likely to identify the correct suspect.

The proportion of correct decisions did not differ significantly for the six-person and three-person groups. Accordingly, Figure 3.2 gives the proportion of correct decisions for the members and groups for the four conditions of shared or profile information and solve or judge set. Over shared and profile conditions 67% of the group decisions were correct for solve set and 33% for judge set, supporting the authors' prediction. There was no improvement from the member decisions to the group decision in the profile (unshared) and judge set condition, whereas the group decisions were more accurate than the member decisions in each of the other three conditions.

Social Validation of Information

In studies of unshared information only one group member has previously seen the information that leads to an optimal decision, whereas all members have seen the information that leads to a suboptimal decision. Thus the group members can mutually validate the shared information but cannot validate the unshared information. Stasser, Stewart,

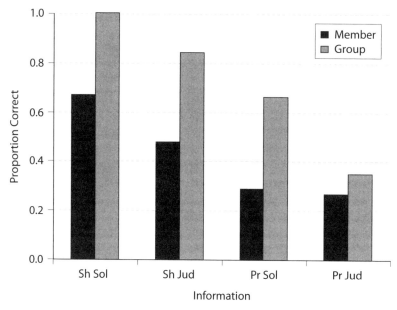

Figure 3.2. Proportion of Correct Responses for Shared (Sh) versus Profile (Pr) Information and Solve (Sol) versus Judge (Jud) Instructions (Stasser and Stewart 1992)

and Wittenbaum (1995) reasoned that instructions for each member to concentrate on learning the information about one suspect (Member X and Suspect A, Member Y and Suspect B, Member Z and Suspect C) would make each person a recognized "expert" on one suspect, so that the expert would be more likely to mention the information and the other members would be more likely to accept it. This should result in a more thorough discussion and a better group decision. Accordingly, they gave expert or no expert instructions. They also forewarned half of the groups that they had unshared information, and did not forewarn the other half. In summary, after the individual decisions the experimental design for the group decision was a 2 × 2 factorial with the variables expert (yes or no) and forewarning (yes or no).

There was no significant difference for the number of correct group decisions for groups that received or did not receive the forewarning instructions. Accordingly, Figure 3.3 gives the proportion of correct group decisions for the members and groups for the expert and no expert instructions, summing over the forewarning conditions. As indicated in Figure 3.3, there were more correct decisions for the groups whose members had received the expert instructions than the groups whose members

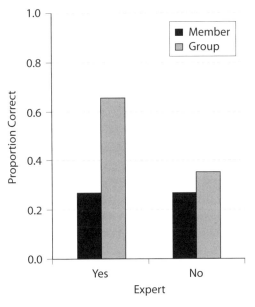

Figure 3.3. Proportion of Correct Decisions for Members Designated as Experts or Not Designated as Experts (Stasser, Stewart, and Wittenbaum 1995)

had not received the expert instructions. The expert groups made better decisions than their members, but the nonexpert groups did not make better decisions than their members. In summary, designating each member as an expert conferred social validation on information possessed only by that person, and hence resulted in better group decisions.

Common Knowledge Effect

Group Judgment

In an experiment by Gigone and Hastie (1993) college students judged the grades obtained by thirty-two introductory psychology students on a scale from A to F (with plusses and minuses) from six predictors: ACT/ SAT percentile, attendance percentage, high school grade point average, enjoyment, other workload, and self-rated anxiety. There were three partially shared cue conditions: (a) two members had three cues, (b) two members had two cues, and (c) two members had one cue. All members had all cues in a shared control condition. On each of the thirty-two items the three members made individual judgments, discussed the item, and then made a group judgment. There was no feedback on the accuracy of the member or group judgments. The influence of each cue was proportional to the number of members who were given the cue. Discussion had no effect other than consolidating the individual member judgments in proportion to the number of members who possessed the cue. In a subsequent study Gigone and Hastie formulated these results as the *Common Knowledge Effect*: "The more group members who know an item of decision-relevant information before discussion, the greater the impact of that information on the group judgment" (1997, p. 132).

Group Choice

In Gigone and Hastie's (1997) subsequent study on group choice, college students chose which of two students had the higher course grade from the same six cues as in the researchers' 1993 study on group judgment. They used the same four conditions of cue distribution over members as were used in the previous study. Again, the three persons made their individual choice, and then discussed the item and made a group choice. The authors predicted that, relative to the previous experiment, "groups making choices will pool information less thoroughly than groups making judgments, but choosers will be more responsive to the implications of information that is pooled" (p. 133).

Gigone and Hastie (1997) proposed a weighted additive model of individual member opinion O:

$$O_A = \Sigma\, u_i\,(c_{1i} - c_{2i}) + e$$

O_A: opinion of member A
i: each cue in available set of cues
u_i: member weight on ith cue value difference
c_{1i} and c_{2i}: choice options 1 and 2 for cue i
e: unmodeled error

They tested three models of the group choice G:

(1) Majority social combination rule

$$G = O_M + e'$$

(2) Combination of the cue value differences:

$$G = \Sigma\, v_i\,(c_{1i} - c_{2i}) + e''$$

v_i: group weight on ith cue value difference

(3) Both member opinions and cue value differences:

$$G = tO_M + \Sigma\, w_i\,(c_{1i} - c_{2i}) + e'''$$

t: group weight on majority member choice
w_i: group weight on ith cue value difference

In analyzing the data Gigone and Hastie regressed group choice of Student 1 or Student 2 on the difference between the student values on each of the six cues across the thirty-two choices separately for each of forty groups. The regression coefficients were standardized and averaged across groups in each of the four conditions to give a condition mean total cue impact for each of the six cues. Then they determined the linear trend and the quadratic trend for cues shared by three, two, or one members.

There were four major results. First, the linear trend was significant for four of six cues. This demonstrates the common knowledge effect. Second, the group choices were more accurate than the average member choice for the percentage of correct choices (of thirty-two). Third, the cues had more impact on the group choice when they were known by two or three group members before discussion than when they were known only by a single group member, independent of their validity for the choice. Fourth, these choice groups placed more weight on the most prominent cue and less weight on the other five cues relative to the judgment groups in the previous experiment.

In summary, the more group members who know an item of information before discussion, the greater the impact of that information on both group judgment and group choice. The common knowledge effect therefore demonstrates the importance of group memory. Although the judgments of the student grades and the choice of the better of two students had correct answers, because of differences in member learning and weighting of the importance of the cues the correct answers in this research tradition are closer to the judgmental end of the intellective judgmental continuum and less demonstrable than the world knowledge and problem-solving tasks in the research we consider in the following chapters.

JURY MEMORY

Hastie, Penrod, and Pennington (1983) conducted an extensive and realistic study of experimental juries in a criminal murder case. The participants were citizens who had been called for a month of jury duty in Cambridge, Massachusetts, and agreed to participate in an experiment when they were not serving in actual trials. After individually watching a three-hour videotaped reenactment of a murder trial, they decided among the four possible verdicts of first degree murder, second degree murder, manslaughter, or not guilty by reason of self-defense. Then they took a recall memory test for items of evidence from the trial and the instructions of the judge for the four verdict categories, such as the legal meaning of premeditation, malice, self-defense, and reasonable doubt. Next they deliberated in twelve-person juries to decide on one of the four possible verdicts. These deliberations were videotaped.

The individual probability of correctly recalling the evidence was .60, and the individual probability of correctly recalling the instructions of the judge was .45. Analyses of the videotaped jury deliberations indicated that the jury probability of correctly recalling the evidence was .92, and the probability of correctly recalling the instructions on the verdict categories was .82. Thus the jury memory was considerably better than the average memory of the jury members, supporting one of the reasons for using juries given by the Supreme Court (*Ballew v. Georgia* 1978). Devine et al. (2001) summarize other evidence for the effectiveness of jury relative to juror memory.

In addition to the information presented in the trial, Hastie, Penrod, and Pennington (1983) found that the jury members made inferences based on their previous world knowledge. This is a type of memory-based problem solving. Research on group problem solving on world knowledge tasks is considered in the following chapter.

SUMMARY

Group memory may be both an end in itself and a necessary preliminary process for further group problem solving. Research on group recognition memory indicates that group memory is better than the memory of the average individual. Transactive memory systems are based on previous shared encoding and storage of information, motivated by cognitive interdependence and convergent expectations, and may facilitate collective memory retrieval both as a process in itself and a necessary process for further problem solving. Assigning different information to be learned by different group members is more effective than having all members learn all information. Research on shared versus unshared information indicates that groups are more likely to make correct decisions when they believe they are solving a problem rather than making a judgment. Assigning different members as experts on different response alternatives socially validates information possessed by only one member and thus improves group performance. Thus an important aspect of both transactive memory and unshared information is for the members to know who knows what. Research on the common knowledge effect demonstrates that the more group members who know an item of information before discussion, the greater the impact of that information on both group judgment and group choice. This indicates the importance of supportive group memory on tasks that have correct answers which are difficult to demonstrate. The collective memory of juries is based on both information brought to the trial by the jury members and information in the trial, and is superior to the memory of the average jury member, supporting one of the basic justifications for the use of juries given by the Supreme Court.

Chapter Four

GROUP ABILITY COMPOSITION ON WORLD KNOWLEDGE PROBLEMS

Shaw's (1932) comparison of group versus individual problem solving was followed by further research during the next three decades that concentrated on performance on different types of group tasks. However, there was little research on the ability of the group members relative to the demands of the group task, although the Lorge and Solomon (1955) Model A and Smoke and Zajonc (1962) minimal quorum group decision scheme assumed a truth-wins social combination process and thus emphasized the importance of the ability of the best group members. We now consider research beginning late in this period that systematically varied group ability composition on world knowledge problems.

English Vocabulary

Laughlin, Branch, and Johnson (1969) reported a study that systematically varied the ability composition of three-person groups on English vocabulary problems. In the first part of the study 528 college students from a wide range of courses responded, as individuals, to the vocabulary items of the Terman Concept Mastery Test (Terman 1956). The Terman Concept Mastery Test consists of 115 pairs of words such as "elated and depressed," "flammable and inflammable," "miasma and effluvium," and "disingenuous and artless," and the respondent must decide whether the two words of the pair are synonyms or antonyms. Because there are only two choices (synonym or antonym) the test is scored as the total number of correct items minus the total number of incorrect items to correct for guessing, so that possible scores range from 115 to –115. The 528 scores were rank ordered from highest (113) to lowest (0) and trichotomized into high (H), medium (M), and low (L) thirds.

The respondents were then assigned to one of the ten possible compositions of H, M, and L members for the second administration of the same test: HHH (three members from the high third), HHM (two members from the high third and one from the middle third), HHL, HMM, HML, HLL, MMM, MML, MLL, and LLL. The group members were

TABLE 4.1
Mean Performance on Second Administration of Part 1
of Terman Concept Mastery Test (Maximum = 115)
for Three-Person Groups and Control Individuals

Condition	Mean	Comparison
HHH	80	
HHM	74	
HHL	67	A
HML	64	AB
HMM	61	B
H	60	BC
HLL	56	C
MMM	48	D
M	42	DE
MML	39	E
MLL	37	E
L	25	F
LLL	21	F

Note: In the comparison column means not sharing a common letter differ significantly.

Source: Laughlin, Branch, and Johnson 1969.

not informed of their scores on the first administration. The groups were instructed to discuss each item and come to a group decision. No decision rule (unanimity, majority, etc.) was imposed or implied, and if a group asked what decision rule to use they were told it was up to them. Control H, M, and L individuals took the same test alone the second time, both to assess learning over the two administrations and to provide a basis of comparison with groups of different ability levels.

Table 4.1 gives the mean number of correct items minus incorrect items (rounded to whole numbers) on the second administration of the Terman vocabulary items for the ten types of groups and the H, M, and L control individuals. The results of the seventy-eight possible pairwise comparisons (HHH vs. HHM, etc.) are given in the third column of Table 4.1. Means that do not share a common letter (for example, HHH and HHM) differ significantly, whereas means that share a common letter (for example, HHL and HML) do not differ significantly.

In general, performance was proportional to the number of high-ability group members. The HHH groups with three members performed better than all the other twelve conditions, including the H individuals. The HHM and HHL groups with two high-ability members performed better than all conditions with one high-ability member or no high-ability member, except for a nonsignificant difference between the HHL and HML groups. The three groups with one high member (HMM, HML, and HLL) and the H individuals performed better than any group without a high-ability member. The MMM groups with three medium-ability members performed better than the MML and MLL groups, which did not differ from each other. The HHH groups performed better than the H individuals, but the MMM groups did not differ from the M individuals, and the LLL groups did not differ from the L individuals.

In summary, these results clearly indicate the importance of the ability composition of the group members on these difficult world knowledge vocabulary items. Performance was generally proportional to the number of high-ability group members. Groups of three high-ability members performed considerably better than the high-ability individuals, but groups of three medium-ability members did not perform better than the medium-ability individuals, and groups of three low-ability members did not perform better than the low-ability individuals. This indicates a greater heterogeneity of member ability at the high-ability level than the medium-ability and low-ability levels.

In a subsequent study Laughlin and Branch (1972) compared the fifteen combinations of four-person groups of high ability, medium ability, and low ability on the same Terman vocabulary items. The participants were 1,008 undergraduate and graduate students from a wide range of courses. After they took the vocabulary items as individuals, the 1,008 scores were rank ordered from highest (107) to lowest (-17). The participants were then assigned to one of the fifteen possible compositions of high, medium, and low members or control individual conditions for the second administration of the same vocabulary items: HHHH, HHHM, HHHL, HHMM, HHML, HHLL, HMMM, HMML, HMLL, HLLL, MMMM, MMML, MMLL, MLLL, LLLL, H, M, and L.

Table 4.2 gives the mean number of correct items minus incorrect items (rounded to whole numbers) on the second administration of the Terman vocabulary items for the fifteen types of groups and H, M, and L control individuals. The results of the 153 pairwise comparisons are given in the third column of Table 4.2. Means that do not share a common letter (for example, HHHM and HHMM) differ significantly, whereas means that share a common letter (for example, HHHH and HHHM) do not differ significantly.

Performance for the groups was generally proportional to the number of high-ability group members. The HHHH, HHHM, and HHHL groups with four or three high-ability members performed better than any group with two or fewer high-ability members. Similarly, the HHMM, HHML, and HHLL groups with two high-ability members performed better than any group with no high-ability members. The HMMM, HMML, HMLL,

TABLE 4.2
Mean Performance on Second Administration
of Part 1 of Terman Concept Mastery Test

Condition	Mean	Comparison
HHHH	81	A
HHHL	75	A
HHHM	74	A
HHMM	63	B
H	62	B
HHML	60	B
HHLL	60	B
HMMM	55	BC
HMML	54	BC
HMLL	48	CD
HLLL	48	CD
MMMM	48	CD
MMML	42	DE
MMLL	39	DE
MLLL	37	EF
M	33	EF
LLLL	26	FG
L	21	G

Note: In the comparison column means not sharing a common letter
differ significantly.
Source: Laughlin and Branch 1972.

and HLLL groups with one high-ability member performed better than
all groups with no high-ability members except MMMM.

The H high-ability individuals performed as well as the HHMM,
HHML, and HHLL groups with two high-ability members, and as well
as the HMMM and HMML groups with one high-ability member. Thus
the medium-ability members contributed little to a group with one high-
ability member. The high-ability individuals performed better than all
groups without a high-ability member. The high-ability individuals performed better than the HMLL and HLLL groups, indicating that the
low-ability members of these groups detracted from what the high-ability
member would have done alone.

The HHHH, HHHM, and HHHL groups with four or three high-
ability members performed better than the H individuals. The MMMM
groups with four medium-ability members performed better than the M
individuals, but the MMML, MMLL, and MLLL groups did not perform
better than the M individuals. The LLLL groups with four low-ability

members did not perform better than the L low-ability individuals. Thus the superiority of group over individual problem solving improved with the ability level of the group members: both groups with three and four high-ability members performed better than they would alone, only groups with four medium-ability members performed better than they would alone, and four groups with four low-ability members did not perform better than they would alone.

In the two previous studies medium-ability groups performed more like low-ability groups than high-ability groups. Moreover, there was some suggestion that three-person and four-person groups of high-ability members did not differ across the two studies. Accordingly, Laughlin et al. (1975) gave the Terman vocabulary items to individuals and then dichotomized at the median to compose high-ability and low-ability groups of sizes two, three, four, and five and control high-ability and low-ability individuals for the second administration of the vocabulary items.

Means for the groups and individuals on the second administration are given in Table 4.3. As indicated in Table 4.3, the performance of the high-ability groups increased directly with group size, and all pairs of means differed significantly except sizes three (HHH) and four (HHHH). In contrast, there was not a significant effect of increasing group size for the low-ability groups. There was a large difference between the high-ability five-person groups and the high-ability control individuals but relatively little difference between the low-ability five-person groups and the low-ability control individuals. Moreover, a high-ability individual performed significantly better than low-ability groups of sizes two, three, four, and five.

What social combination processes underlie these results? Table 4.4 gives five social combination models formalizing possible group processes for the five-person groups. We have already considered the majority, truth-supported wins, and truth-wins models in chapter 3. The

TABLE 4.3

Mean Performance on Second Administration of Part 1 of Terman Concept Mastery Test (Maximum = 115) for High-Ability and Low-Ability Groups of Sizes Two, Three, Four, and Five and Control Individuals

	Size				
	One	Two	Three	Four	Five
High-Ability	53	60	67	69	76
Low-Ability	23	26	27	31	32

Source: Laughlin et al. 1975.

TABLE 4.4
Majority, Proportionality, Equiprobability, Truth-Supported
Wins, and Truth-Wins Models for Five-Person Groups

Members		Maj		Prop		Equi		TSW		TW	
Cor	Inc	Cor	Inc	Cor	Inc	Cor	Inc	Cor	Inc	Cor	Inc
5	0	1.00	.00	1.00	.00	1.00	.00	1.00	.00	1.00	.00
4	1	1.00	.00	.80	.20	.50	.50	1.00	.00	1.00	.00
3	2	1.00	.00	.60	.40	.50	.50	1.00	.00	1.00	.00
2	3	.00	1.00	.40	.60	.50	.50	1.00	.00	1.00	.00
1	4	.00	1.00	.20	.80	.50	.50	.00	1.00	1.00	.00
0	5	.00	1.00	.00	1.00	.00	1.00	.00	1.00	.00	1.00

Note: Maj = Majority; Prop = Proportionality; Equi = Equiprobability; TSW = Truth-Supported Wins; TW = Truth Wins; Cor = Correct; Inc = Incorrect.
Source: Laughlin et al. 1975.

proportionality model formalizes a process where the group decision corresponds to the proportion of group members who favor each response. For example, if three members favor the correct response and two members favor the incorrect response, the predicted probability of a correct group response is 3/5 = .60, and the predicted probability of an incorrect group response is 2/5 = .40. The equiprobability model proposes that the group response is equally probable among any responses proposed by at least one group member. Thus it predicts a probability of 1.00 of the correct response when only the correct response is proposed in the 5-0 distribution, and a probability of 1.00 of the incorrect response when only the incorrect response is proposed in the 0-5 distribution. In the other four distributions where at least one member proposes the correct response and at least one member proposes the incorrect response there is a predicted probability of .50 of each of the correct and incorrect responses. The best-fitting social decision scheme for the five-person high-ability groups was truth-supported wins, and the other four models could be rejected. All five models were rejected for the low-ability groups.

Table 4.5 gives the majority, proportionality, equiprobability, truth-supported wins, and truth-wins models for four-person groups. The best fitting model for both high-ability and low-ability groups was truth-supported wins, and the other models were rejected. The best-fitting model for the three-person high-ability groups was also truth-supported wins. However, the best-fitting model for the three-person low-ability groups was proportionality. This fit of the proportionality model means that the groups simply recovered the member preference distribution (as would happen if they wrote each person's preference on a card, put all

TABLE 4.5

Majority, Proportionality, Equiprobability, Truth-Supported Wins, and Truth-Wins Social Decision Schemes (Combination Models) for Four-Person Groups

Members		Maj		Prop		Equi		TSW		TW	
Cor	Inc	Cor	Inc	Cor	Inc	Cor	Inc	Cor	Inc	Cor	Inc
4	0	1.00	.00	1.00	.00	1.00	.00	1.00	.00	1.00	.00
3	1	1.00	.00	.75	.25	.50	.50	1.00	.00	1.00	.00
2	2	.50	.50	.50	.50	.50	.50	1.00	.00	1.00	.00
1	3	.00	1.00	.25	.75	.50	.50	.00	1.00	1.00	.00
0	4	.00	1.00	.00	1.00	.00	1.00	.00	1.00	.00	1.00

Note: Maj = Majority; Prop = Proportionality; Equi = Equiprobability; TSW = Truth-Supported Wins; TW = Truth Wins; Cor = Correct; Inc = Incorrect.

Source: Laughlin et al. 1975.

the cards in a hat, and drew an unseen card at random), with no improvement over their members. This is consistent with the finding that the three-person medium-ability groups (MMM) did not differ from the M individuals in the previous study of Laughlin, Branch, and Johnson (1969) (see Table 4.1).

In summary, the basic social combination process was truth-supported wins, where two correct group members are necessary and sufficient for a correct group response. Truth-supported wins was the best-fitting model for each of five-person, four-person, and three-person high-ability groups, and for four-person low-ability groups. One correct member in the group was not sufficient for a correct group response, as in the Lorge and Solomon Model A and the Smoke and Zajonc minimum quorum group decision scheme. Incorrect majorities prevailed over one correct group member, but not over two correct group members. All models were rejected for five-person low-ability groups, and all models but proportionality were rejected for three-person low-ability groups.

Laughlin et al. (1976) extended research on group ability composition to two further types of world knowledge problems for the same four-person groups in one study, The first type of problems was the general achievement items of the Otis Quick-Scoring Mental Ability Test (Otis 1954). This Otis Test consists of vocabulary, analogy, mathematics, reasoning, and general information items. The second type of problems was the Mednick and Mednick Remote Associates Test (Mednick and Mednick 1967). This Remote Associates Test consists of thirty sets of three words that can be related by a fourth word which the respondent must supply, such as "athletes," "web," and "rabbit," for which the answer is "foot."

Five hundred high-school students took both the Otis and the Mednick and Mednick tests as individuals. The scores for each test were then dichotomized at the median to define high-ability (H) and low-ability (L). The students then retook the Otis and the Mednick as cooperative groups in one of three ability combinations: (1) four high-ability members on both tests, (2) two high-ability members and two low-ability members on both tests, (3) four low-ability members on both tests. (A few students who were high-ability on one test and low-ability on the other were assigned to the condition they most closely approximated.) Control H and L individuals retook each test a second time alone. We first consider performance on the Otis general achievement test, and then performance on the Mednick and Mednick Remote Associates test.

General Achievement

Because the Otis general achievement test included vocabulary, analogies, and other world knowledge items of moderate to high demonstrability the authors predicted that performance would improve with the number of high-ability group members and that the best-fitting social combination model would be truth-supported wins.

Table 4.6 gives the mean performance of the groups and individuals on the second administration. As indicated in Table 4.6, performance was directly proportional to the number of high-ability members of the group. The HHHH groups with four high-ability members performed better than the HHLL groups with two high-ability members, and both HHHH and HHLL groups performed better than the H individuals. The

Table 4.6
Mean Performance (Maximum = 80) on Second
Administration of Otis Achievement Test for
Four-Person Groups and Control Individuals

Condition	Mean	Comparison
HHHH	73	
HHLL	67	
H	62	
LLLL	56	
L	49	

Note: In the comparison column means not sharing a common letter differ significantly.
Source: Laughlin et al. 1976.

H individuals performed better than both the LLLL groups with four low-ability members and the L individuals, and the LLLL groups performed better than the L individuals. The best-fitting of the five social combination models of Table 4.5 was truth-supported wins for each of the HHHH, HHLL, and LLLL groups, extending the truth-supported-wins process to another type of world knowledge problems.

REMOTE VERBAL ASSOCIATIONS

The Mednick and Mednick (1967) items were developed to assess an associative theory of the creative process and were chosen so that the correct answers would be immediately obvious once proposed (an insight or Eureka task). Thus the authors predicted that the best-fitting social combination model would be truth wins for each of the HHHH, HHLL, and LLLL conditions.

Table 4.7 gives the mean performance of the groups and individuals on the second administration. As indicated in Table 4.7, the HHHH groups with four high-ability members and the HHLL groups with two high-ability members did not differ significantly from each other, and both performed better than the LLLL groups, the H individuals, and the L individuals. The H individuals did not differ from the LLLL groups and performed better than the L individuals. The LLLL groups with four low-ability members performed better than the L individuals. The best-fitting social combination model for each of the HHHH, HHLL, and LLLL groups was truth wins.

TABLE 4.7
Mean Performance (Maximum = 30) on Second
Administration of Mednick and Mednick Remotes Associates
Test for Four-Person Groups and Control Individuals

Condition	Mean	Comparison
HHHH	27	A
HHLL	24	A
LLLL	21	B
H	20	B
L	12	

Note: In the comparison column means not sharing a common letter differ significantly.

Source: Laughlin et al. 1976.

Unlike the previous studies with vocabulary and general achievement world knowledge items, groups of four high-ability members did not perform better than groups with two high-ability members and two low-ability members. This reflects the strong truth-wins process, where only one correct member is necessary for a correct group response, in contrast to the two correct members who are necessary for vocabulary and general achievement world knowledge items. Both the HHHH and LLLL groups performed better than their respective H and L individual controls, indicating the effectiveness of groups relative to individuals at both ability levels.

Homogeneity and Heterogeneity of Group Member Ability

A general question in small group performance is homogeneity and heterogeneity of member characteristics. Will groups with homogeneous (similar) or heterogeneous (dissimilar) members perform better? Obviously, when this general question of homogeneity versus heterogeneity is posed, the particular ability, personality, or demographic characteristic must be specified. Less obviously, the basis of comparison that defines groups as homogeneous or heterogeneous must be specified—for example, given a population whose members differ on a dimension such as ability, one must ask homogeneous or heterogeneous in relation to what.

Assume a distribution of individual ability. If we trichotomize the distribution into high (H), medium (M), and low (L) thirds and compose three-person groups, the most heterogeneous group is HML. The three types of homogeneous groups are HHH, MMM, and LLL. The six other types of mixed groups, with two members of one third and one member of another third (HHM, HHL, HMM, HLL, MML, and MLL) are less heterogeneous than HML but more heterogeneous than HHH, MMM, and LLL.

The previous research indicates that HHH groups performed considerably better than H individuals, whereas MMM groups did not perform better than M individuals and LLL groups did not perform better than L individuals. The reason seems to be much greater heterogeneity of ability across the different items within the HHH groups than within the MMM and LLL groups. Similarly, the four-person HHHH groups performed considerably better than the H individuals, the MMMM groups performed only somewhat better than the M individuals, and the LLLL groups did not perform better than the L individuals. Within the overall high third of the ability distributions in these studies, different individuals were heterogeneous in relationship to one another: different individuals had different information that other individuals did not have. Thus they were able to pool information and performed better as a group than they would have performed separately. Within the overall low third of the ability distribution, different individuals were homogeneous in relationship to one another: one low-ability individual had substantially the same information as other low-ability individuals, so they were not able to pool information and performed no better together than they would have performed separately. Within the middle third of the ability distribution, the individuals were somewhat heterogeneous in relationship to one another, so that groups of four medium members were able to perform better than the medium individuals, but groups of three medium members were not.

Thus, in a comparison of homogeneous and heterogeneous groups, the overall ability level of the homogeneous groups must be specified. Homogeneous high-ability groups of sizes three or four have been demonstrated to perform considerably better than heterogeneous groups of the same size. HHH groups have performed better than HMM, HML, or HLL groups; and HHHH groups have performed better than HHML, HMMM, HMML, HMLL, or LLLL groups. In contrast, homogeneous low-ability groups of size three or four have been demonstrated to perform considerably worse than heterogeneous groups of the same size; LLL groups have performed worse than HMM, HML, and HLL groups; and LLLL groups have performed worse than HHMM, HHML, HHLL, HMMM, or HMML groups. The best explanation of all these results is that performance is proportional to the number of high-ability group members. In terms of homogeneity and heterogeneity of member ability, homogeneously high-ability groups perform better than heterogeneous or mixed-ability groups, and homogeneously low-ability groups perform worse than heterogeneous or mixed-ability groups.

Conclusions on Group Ability Composition

On difficult world knowledge tasks, high-ability persons performed better in cooperative groups with other high-ability members than they did alone, and this difference increased with group size. In contrast, low-ability persons did not perform better in cooperative groups with other low-ability members than they did alone, and there was little improvement as group size increased. Low-ability members contributed very little unique information to one another and virtually none to high-ability members. Medium-ability members displayed an intermediate pattern that was more like low-ability than high-ability members: groups of four medium-ability members performed better than medium-ability individuals, but groups of two or three medium-ability members did not perform better than medium-ability individuals. Consequently the performance of groups of mixed high-ability, medium-ability, and low-ability members was basically proportional to the number of high-ability members: the greater the proportion of high-ability members, the better the group performance.

The designations "high-ability," "medium-ability," and "low-ability" are not fixed characteristics of the participants such as brown eyes or tonsils, where a given person has or does not have the characteristic regardless of the number of other people who have or do not have the characteristic. Rather, high-ability, medium-ability, and low-ability were defined by trichotomization of the distribution of participants so that a given participant was high, medium, or low relative to other participants rather than possessing a fixed characteristic. The participants in the bottom third of these distributions were intelligent, motivated, and successful students with considerable world knowledge and might well be considered "high-ability" relative to a less educated population.

Analogously, an NFL professional football team has a starting quarterback, a first backup quarterback, and a second backup quarterback, who, relative to one another, may be called high, medium, and low, although all three are exceptional relative to the college quarterbacks who never made the roster of an NFL team. There are many fine violin players who do not perform with world-class symphony orchestras. Although they may be "medium" or "low" relative to these exceptional violinists, they may well be "high" relative to many other violinists. Group ability composition in the studies in this chapter was not a fixed characteristic of the participants but was relative to the other members of their group, relative to the other groups, and relative to the difficulty of the problems. With these qualifications, the results for group ability composition in these studies should generalize to other populations and world knowledge problems.

Chapter Five

COLLECTIVE INDUCTION

INDUCTION is the search for descriptive, predictive, and explanatory generalizations, rules, and principles. As a psychological process induction begins with the perception of some pattern, regularity, or relationship. A hypothesis or tentative generalization is then formed to account for the regularity. Consideration of the hypothesis suggests predictions, which are then tested by observations and experiments. If the results of observations and experiments support the predictions, the proposed hypothesis becomes more plausible, but if the results of observation and experiment fail to support the predictions, then the hypothesis becomes less plausible and is rejected or revised. Thus the two basic processes in induction are hypothesis formation (observation of a regularity and proposal of a tentative generalization) and hypothesis evaluation (test of predictions from the hypothesis by observation and experiment).

This inductive process occurs for both single individuals and cooperative groups such as scientific research teams, auditing teams, securities and intelligence analysts, art experts, or air crash investigators. In such cooperative groups different members or subgroups of members may perceive regularities, propose hypotheses, reject hypotheses that are not consistent with the evidence, derive predictions, test the predictions by observation and experiments, interpret the results, and propose generalizations, rules, or principles. *Collective induction* is the cooperative search for descriptive, predictive, and explanatory generalizations, rules, and principles.

Theoretically collective induction is a divisible and complementary group task (Steiner 1966, 1972) in which groups may perform better than individuals by dividing the task into subtasks and combining the different insights, understandings, strategies, and other cognitive processes of the group members. Groups may recognize patterns and relationships collectively that none of their members recognize individually. They may propose correct emergent group responses that no group member had previously proposed. Do such processes, in fact, occur in collective induction so that collective induction is superior to individual induction? We first describe a rule-learning task for collective induction. We then report a series of experiments with this task.

An Inductive Rule-Learning Task

The objective is to induce a rule that partitions ordinary playing cards of four suits (clubs, diamonds, hearts, and spades) and thirteen cards per suit (ace, deuce, trey, . . . , king) into examples and nonexamples of the rule. Aces are assigned the numerical value 1, deuces 2, treys 3, . . . , tens 10, jacks 11, queens 12, and kings 13. The rule may be based on any characteristics of the cards, such as suit (e.g., diamonds or spades), number (e.g., eights, jacks, or multiples of three), or any numerical and/or logical operations on suit and number of any degree of complexity (e.g., diamond or spade jacks; diamonds eight and above or spades seven and below; two clubs alternate with two hearts; two even clubs alternate with two odd hearts).

The instructions to the groups explain that the objective is to induce a rule that partitions ordinary playing cards into examples and non-examples of the rule in as few trials as possible. The instructions explain the meaning of a rule, the assignment of numbers to cards (ace = 1, deuce = 2, etc.), and the procedure. The instructions explain that the rule may be based on any characteristics of the cards such as numerical value, color, suit, logical connectives, alternation, or any combinations of these, and give illustrations of a number of rules of various types. The problem begins by placing on the table a known positive example of the rule, such as the eight of diamonds for the rule "two diamonds alternate with two clubs." A trial consists of the following four stages: first, each group member writes his or her hypothesis (proposed correct rule) on a member hypothesis sheet; second, the group members engage in discussion until they reach a consensus on a group hypothesis, which a randomly selected group member writes on another group hypothesis sheet; third, the group members reach a consensus on the play of any of the fifty-two cards and show it to the experimenter; and fourth, the experimenter classifies the card as either an example or a nonexample of the correct rule. Examples are placed to the right of the known example on the table, and non-examples are placed below the known example. As this cycle continues on successive trials, a progressive array of examples and nonexamples develops in the order of play. There are ten trials of hypotheses and card plays, with no feedback on either member or group hypothesis until after ten trials. Table 5.1 illustrates an array of card plays and hypotheses for the correct rule "two diamonds alternate with two clubs."

Collective versus Individual Induction:
Effects of Increasing Evidence

Over the past seventy-five years a large number of experiments have consistently found that group problem solving is superior to individual

TABLE 5.1.
Illustration of Card Plays and Hypotheses for One Array

		Card Plays			
8D	6D	2C	8C	6D	2D
	9H	2H		4C	
	8H				
	4D				

Hypothesis 1: Even diamonds (after known example of 8D)
Hypothesis 2: Red (after first card play of 6D)
Hypothesis 3: Diamonds (after second card play of 9H)
Hypothesis 4: Diamonds
Hypothesis 5: Diamonds six and above and clubs
Hypothesis 6: Diamonds and clubs
Hypothesis 7: Even diamonds and even clubs
Hypothesis 8: Two red alternate with two black
Hypothesis 9: Diamonds six and above and all clubs
Hypothesis 10: Two even diamonds alternate with two even clubs
Final Hypothesis: Two diamonds alternate with two clubs (after last card play)

Source: Laughlin, VanderStoep, and Hollingshead 1991.

problem solving (recall the references in chapter 2). This research has typically compared *N* groups of size *S* and *N* individuals, such as twenty-four groups of size four and twenty-four individuals. With random assignment to group and individual conditions this compares groups and the *average* individual. There are three explanations for this superiority: (a) groups recognize and reject errors (dating from Shaw 1932); (b) groups recognize and adopt correct responses if proposed by at least one group member (dating from Lorge and Solomon 1955); and (c) groups process more information than individuals (e.g., Hinsz, Tindale, and Vollrath 1997).

Although it is theoretically a divisible complementary task on which groups should perform better than individuals, is collective induction, in fact, superior to individual induction? Laughlin, VanderStoep, and Hollingshead (1991) compared twenty-four groups of size four and 24 × 4 = 96 individuals for each of one, two, three, and four arrays of hypotheses and card choices (one array is illustrated in Table 5.1) on the rule-learning task. This allows comparison of the twenty-four groups with the twenty-four best, twenty-four second-best, twenty-four third-best, and twenty-four fourth-best individuals, and is thus a more stringent comparison of group versus individual problem solving than comparison of groups and average individuals.

The experiment investigated the third explanation of superior group performance that groups collectively process more information than individuals by varying four levels of potential information. In the first level of potential information, the group or individual proposed one hypothesis and played one card on each of the ten trials and then proposed their final hypothesis, as described previously and illustrated in Table 5.1. In the second level of potential information, the group or individual proposed one hypothesis and played one card on each of two separate arrays on each trial. Instructions indicated that they were solving only one rule from the two separate arrays. The initial known example was the same on both arrays. The hypotheses and card plays could be the same or different on the two arrays on the first ten trials, but the final hypothesis had to be the same on both arrays. Table 5.2 provides an illustration for the correct rule "two diamonds and two clubs alternate." Note that the known initial example, the eight of diamonds, is the same for both arrays. In the illustration, the hypothesis "red cards" is proposed and the 10D is played on the first trial on the first array, and the hypothesis "even diamonds" is proposed and the 6D is played on the first trial on the second array. The final hypothesis, "two diamonds alternate with two clubs" was, as required, the same on both arrays, and was correct. Similarly, in the third and fourth levels of potential information, the group or individual proposed one hypothesis and played one card on each of three or four separate arrays on each trial.

If the group or individual propose the same hypothesis and play the same card on the first trial on each of the two, three, or four arrays, the information is totally redundant, and they obviously receive no more information from two, three, or four arrays than from one. However, if they propose different hypotheses on the different arrays, play different cards, or both, they may receive more information from two, three, or four arrays than from one. Thus the experimental manipulation of the amount of potential information tested the theoretical possibility that the superiority of collective induction over individual induction is because of the superiority of collective information processing over individual information processing.

The participants were 768 college students in psychology classes. Half were randomly assigned to solve the problems as a cooperative four-person group and the other half as individuals. The group or individuals solved the problems from one, two, three, or four arrays. There were twenty-four correct rules, all involving alternation over four or five cards, such as two diamonds alternate with two clubs, or two spades alternate with three hearts.

The first, second, third, and fourth individuals for each of the twenty-four rules within each array condition were defined by their proportion of correct hypotheses. Figure 5.1 shows the proportions of correct

TABLE 5.2
Illustration of Card Plays and Hypotheses for Two Arrays

Array One	8D	10D	7C	KC	2D	QD		
			6H	QH				
			4S					
			AD					
			6D					

1. red cards
2. all diamonds and clubs greater than 6
3. odd to even
4. hearts to spades
5. diamonds and clubs
6. all diamonds and clubs greater than 5
7. all diamonds and clubs greater than 5
8. all diamonds and clubs greater than 5
9. two even diamonds alternate with two odd clubs
10. two even diamonds alternate with two odd clubs
Final Hypothesis: two diamonds alternate with two clubs

Array Two	8D	6D	4C	7C	2D	7D	KC	JC
		5H	AH					
		2S						

1. even diamonds
2. even diamonds and hearts below 6
3. two red then one black
4. even diamonds and clubs
5. even numbers
6. even numbers
7. even numbers
8. two diamonds alternate with two clubs
9. two diamonds alternate with two clubs
10. two diamonds alternate with two clubs
Final Hypothesis: two diamonds alternate with two clubs

Note: Correct rule is two diamonds alternate with two clubs.
Source: Laughlin, VanderStoep, and Hollingshead 1991.

hypotheses for the groups and first, second, third, and fourth individuals for each of one, two, three, and four arrays. As evident in Figure 5.1 and confirmed by Newman-Keuls comparisons, the first individuals had a higher proportion of correct hypotheses than the groups or second, third, or fourth individuals. The groups and second individuals did not

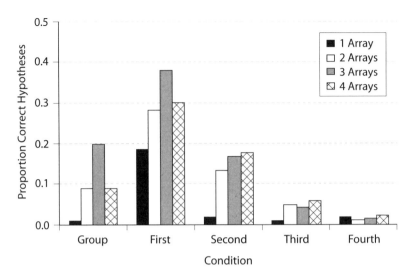

Figure 5.1. Proportion of Correct Hypotheses Experiment 1 (Laughlin, VanderStoep, and Hollingshead 1991)

differ significantly. Both the groups and second individuals had a higher proportion of correct hypotheses than both the third and fourth individuals, who did not differ significantly from each other.

As indicated in Figure 5.1, there were similar curvilinear patterns for both the group and first individuals, with more correct hypotheses for two and three arrays than for one and four arrays. The second individuals had more correct hypotheses for each of two, three, and four arrays than for one array and no differences between two, three, and four arrays. There was little difference between one, two, three, and four arrays for the third and fourth individuals. This indicates that the groups and first individuals were able to process the additional information from two and three arrays; the second individuals could process the additional information from two arrays; and the third and fourth individuals were not able to process further potential information in additional arrays.

Nonplausible hypotheses are inconsistent with the evidence, such as the hypothesis "hearts" when a heart has been a nonexample or the hypothesis "spades" when a diamond has been an example. Figure 5.2 gives the proportions of nonplausible hypotheses. Figures 5.1 and 5.2 indicate that the proportion of correct hypotheses for the groups decreased, but the proportions of nonplausible hypotheses did not increase from three to four arrays. This suggests that the groups may have been able to profit from the additional potential information from three to four arrays but did not have sufficient time to do so. Accordingly, Experiment 2 used five

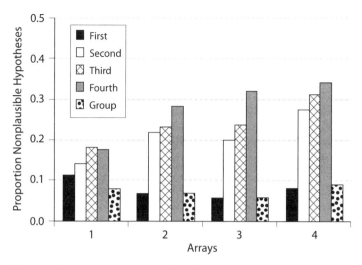

Figure 5.2. Proportion of Nonplausible Hypotheses Experiment 1 (Laughlin, VanderStoep, and Hollingshead 1991)

arrays and allowed ten more minutes to solve the problem. Given the additional time, the groups were predicted to perform at the level of the best (first) individuals for both the proportion of correct hypotheses and the proportion of nonplausible hypotheses.

The participants in Experiment 2 were 144 college students. Half were randomly assigned to solve rule induction problems as a cooperative four-person group (eighteen groups) and the other half as individuals (seventy-two individuals). The group or individuals solved the problem from five arrays. Figure 5.3 gives the proportions of correct and nonplausible hypotheses for the groups and first, second, third, and fourth individuals. As indicated in Figure 5.3, the groups had approximately the same proportions of correct hypotheses as the first individuals. Both the groups and the first individuals had a higher proportion of correct hypotheses than the second, third, and fourth individuals. The groups had a lower proportion of nonplausible hypotheses than the individuals, and nonplausible hypotheses increased linearly from the first to the fourth individuals.

In summary, in Experiment 1 the groups performed below the level of the first individuals, at the level of the second individuals, and better than the third and fourth individuals in recognizing and adopting correct hypotheses. The groups performed at the level of the first individuals and better than the second, third, and fourth individuals in rejecting nonplausible hypotheses. The proportion of correct hypotheses increased

64   CHAPTER FIVE

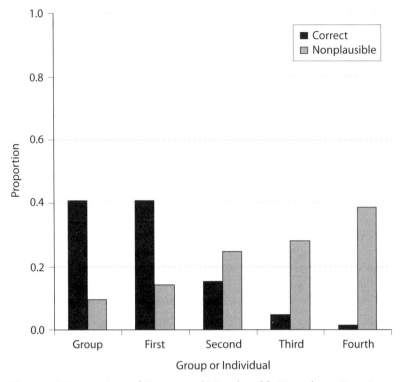

Figure 5.3. Proportions of Correct and Nonplausible Hypotheses Experiment 2 (Laughlin, VanderStoep, and Hollingshead 1991)

with two, three, or four arrays for the groups, first individuals, and second individuals, but not for the third and fourth individuals. The proportion of nonplausible hypotheses did not increase with increasing arrays for the groups, first individuals, or second individuals, but increased from one to two and more arrays for the third and fourth individuals. Thus the groups, first individuals, and second individuals were able to profit from increasing potential information, but the third and fourth individuals were not.

The parallel relationships for the proportion of correct hypotheses for the groups and first individuals in Experiment 1 (Figure 5.1) indicate that group interaction decreased actual group performance from the potential performance of the first group member by a constant amount for each array condition. On average, the best member in each group would be expected to perform as well as the best individuals independently. The results for the third and fourth individuals in Figures 5.1 and 5.2 suggest that the third and fourth members of the groups contributed few correct hypotheses and many nonplausible hypotheses to the group discussion, so that the decreased performance of the groups relative to the expected performance of their best members alone was the result of their third and fourth members.

The findings that the proportion of correct hypotheses decreased from three to four arrays for the groups but the proportion of nonplausible hypotheses did not increase suggested that the groups may have been able to profit from more time with four arrays. Accordingly, Experiment 2 used five arrays and allowed ten more minutes for problem solution. The groups performed at the level of the first individuals and better than the second, third, and fourth individuals for both the proportion of correct hypotheses and the proportion of nonplausible hypotheses. Because the best member of a group frequently cannot be identified prior to group performance and groups are frequently mandated by law, custom, or tradition, this result is of obvious practical as well as theoretical importance.

COLLECTIVE VERSUS INDIVIDUAL INDUCTION: EFFECTS OF INCREASING HYPOTHESES

The previous experiment demonstrated that collective induction is at the level of the best of an equivalent number of individuals, and that performance in collective induction improves with increasing arrays of evidence (card choices) and a single hypothesis on each trial. A related experiment by Laughlin, Bonner, and Altermatt (1998) again compared four-person cooperative groups with an equal number of individuals on rule induction problems.

As in the previous Experiment 1 of Laughlin, VanderStoep, and Hollingshead (1991), the groups or individuals played cards on each of four arrays in the solution of the same rule. The problem began with the same known example of the correct rule on each of the four arrays. In three experimental conditions the groups or individual proposed one hypothesis, two different hypotheses, or four different hypotheses on each trial. In all three conditions they then played any of the fifty-two cards (repetitions allowed) on each of the four arrays. After they had played a card on each of the four arrays the experimenter informed the group or individual whether the selected card was an example or nonexample of the rule on each of the four arrays. The groups or individuals in the two hypotheses and four hypotheses conditions had to propose two different hypotheses or four different hypotheses on each trial. There were no restrictions on card plays on the four arrays. After the tenth trial the group or individual proposed a single final hypothesis. There was no feedback as to whether member or group hypotheses were correct or incorrect until after the final hypothesis. There were sixteen four-person groups and sixty-four individuals in each of the one hypothesis, two hypotheses, and four hypotheses conditions.

The best, second-best, third-best, and fourth-best individuals were determined by the number of correct hypotheses for each rule in each of the one, two, and four hypothesis conditions. Since the groups and individuals in the two hypothesis and four hypothesis conditions had to propose two or four different hypotheses on each trial, only one hypothesis could be correct and the possible number of correct hypotheses therefore ranged from 0 to 11 in all conditions.

Figure 5.4 gives the mean proportions of correct hypotheses. The groups and first individuals did not differ significantly from each other, and both had a higher proportion of correct hypotheses than each of the second, third, and fourth individuals. The effect of one, two, and four hypotheses was not significant. Figure 5.5 gives the proportion of nonplausible hypotheses. The groups and first individuals did not differ significantly from each other, and both had a lower proportion of nonplausible hypotheses than each of the second, third, and fourth individuals. The proportion of nonplausible hypotheses increased linearly with increasing hypotheses: there were more nonplausible hypotheses with two hypotheses than one, and more with four hypotheses than two.

In summary, the four-person groups performed at the level of the best of four independent individuals and better than the second-best, third-best, and fourth-best individuals for both correct hypotheses and nonplausible hypotheses. Together with Experiment 2 of Laughlin, VanderStoep, and Hollingshead (1991) this extends the large literature demonstrating the superiority of groups over the average individual to a comparison of groups and the best, second-best, . . . , Nth best of an equivalent number of N individuals. The two experiments are therefore consistent in finding that groups will perform at the level of the best of an equivalent number of individuals on information-rich induction problems.

These results support the conceptualization of groups as information processors (Hinsz, Tindale, and Vollrath 1997), which emphasizes the capacity of groups to collectively process large amounts of information. This conceptualization subsumes the traditional explanations for group superiority over the average individual in recognizing correct answers and rejecting errors, both of which were supported by the results for correct hypotheses and nonplausible hypotheses, respectively. The large amount of information from four arrays may have resulted in information overload for all but the groups and best individuals. This suggests that groups will be increasingly effective as the complexity, potential information, and sheer size of the problem increases, and that complex problems should be assigned to groups rather than individuals.

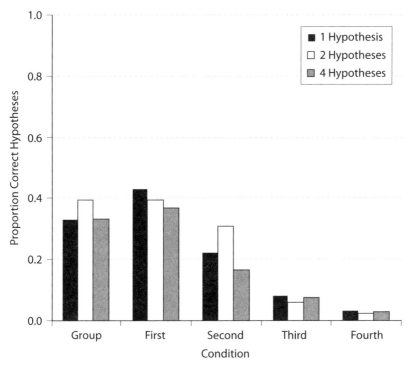

Figure 5.4. Proportion of Correct Hypotheses (Laughlin, Bonner, and Alter-matt 1998)

COLLECTIVE INDUCTION WITH INCREASING
HYPOTHESES AND INCREASING EVIDENCE

The previous research found that collective induction was improved by increasing evidence but not by increasing hypotheses. However, this was for separate experiments rather than within the same experiment. Accordingly, Laughlin and Bonner (1999) conducted a 3 × 3 factorial experiment with the nine combinations of one, two, or four arrays and one, two, or four hypotheses per trial. The subjects were college students in psychology classes. In the nine experimental conditions four-person groups solved rule induction problems from one, two, or four arrays under instructions to propose one hypothesis on each trial, two different hypotheses on each trial, or four different hypotheses on each trial. There were twelve four-person groups in each of the nine experimental conditions.

The groups in the two- and four-hypothesis conditions had to propose two or four different hypotheses on each trial, so that only one of them could be correct. Hence the appropriate measure is the number of trials

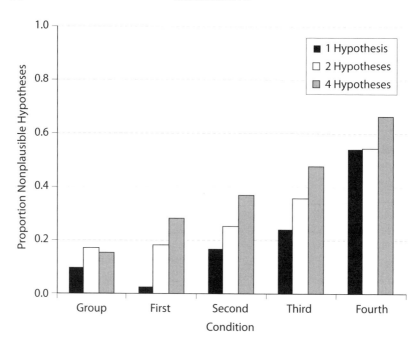

Figure 5.5. Proportion of Nonplausible Hypotheses (Laughlin, Bonner, and Altermatt 1998)

with a correct hypothesis. Figure 5.6 gives the mean proportions of trials with a correct hypothesis. There were significantly more correct hypotheses for both two arrays and four arrays than one array, with a nonsignificant difference between two and four arrays. Thus performance was improved by increasing arrays but not by increasing hypotheses, consistent with previous research that varied either increasing arrays or increasing hypotheses in separate experiments rather than the same experiment (Laughlin, VanderStoep, and Hollingshead 1991; Laughlin, Bonner, and Altermatt 1998).

Figure 5.7 gives the proportion of nonplausible hypotheses. The differences between one, two, and four arrays were not significant. In contrast, the proportion of nonplausible hypotheses increased with increasing proposed hypotheses: there was a higher proportion of nonplausible hypotheses for the two hypothesis condition and a higher proportion for four hypotheses than two.

In summary, the number of correct hypotheses increased from one to two to four arrays but did not differ significantly for one, two, and four

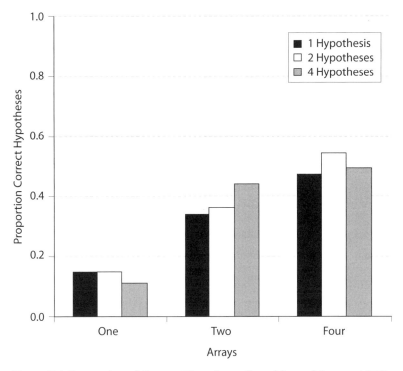

Figure 5.6. Proportion of Correct Hypotheses (Laughlin and Bonner 1999)

hypotheses. The proportion of nonplausible hypotheses increased from one to two to four hypotheses but did not differ significantly for one, two, and four arrays. Increasing evidence resulted in increasing correct hypotheses without a commensurate increase in nonplausible hypotheses. Conversely, increasing hypotheses resulted in increasing nonplausible hypotheses without a commensurate increase in correct hypotheses.

Thus, if a group has sufficient evidence to evaluate hypotheses, then proposing further hypotheses may not only fail to increase correct hypotheses but further increase nonplausible hypotheses. Group interaction virtually assures that the group members will propose multiple hypotheses but they need evidence to evaluate them. An implication of the results of these studies that groups perform at the level of the best of an equivalent number of individuals and that group performance is improved by increasing evidence but not increasing hypotheses is that problems should increasingly be assigned to groups rather than individuals as the complexity of the problem increases.

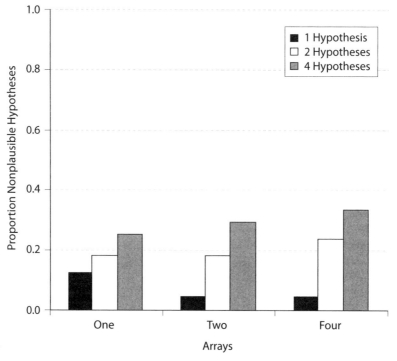

Figure 5.7. Proportion of Nonplausible Hypotheses (Laughlin and Bonner 1999)

POSITIVE HYPOTHESIS TESTS AND NEGATIVE HYPOTHESIS TESTS

Another important issue in collective induction is the effectiveness of positive and negative hypotheses tests. To illustrate, assume that the current hypothesis is "even diamonds." The card play of the eight of diamonds (8D) is a positive hypothesis test, whereas the card play of the seven of diamonds (7D) is a negative hypothesis test. An experiment by Laughlin, Magley, and Shupe (1997) assessed the effectiveness of both positive and negative hypotheses tests. The groups made a hypothesis and played a card on each of four arrays. There were six experimental conditions. In the PPPP Condition the groups were instructed to use a positive test (P) of their current hypothesis on each of the four arrays. In the PPPN Condition the groups were instructed to use positive tests on Arrays 1, 2, and 3, and a negative test (N) on Array 4. In the PPNN Condition the groups were instructed to use positive tests on Arrays 1 and 2, and negative tests on Arrays 3 and 4. In the PNNN Condition the groups were instructed to use a positive test on Array 1 and negative tests on Arrays 2, 3, and 4. In the NNNN Condition the groups were instructed to use negative tests on all arrays. In the Control Condition there were no instructions to use positive or negative hypothesis tests, so the groups could use any combination of positive and negative tests on the four arrays.

The authors proposed that positive tests are more likely to lead to further examples than negative tests, and that examples are more useful than nonexamples in inducing the correct rule because they provide further evidence. Thus the number of correct hypotheses should correspond to the proportion of positive tests on the four arrays.

There were twenty four-person groups in each of the six conditions. The correct rules were alternations of two suits, such as two diamonds alternate with two clubs. After the standard instructions, and depending upon the condition (PPPP, etc.), the experimenter explained the procedure of positive or negative tests of the current group hypothesis on each of the four arrays.

Table 5.3 gives the proportion of examples for each of the four arrays for the six experimental conditions. Inspection of the patterns of significant differences within each array in Table 5.3 indicates the predicted greater probabilities of examples for arrays with instructions to use positive tests than for arrays with instructions to use negative tests. These results support the prediction that positive hypothesis tests will be more likely to be followed by an example than negative hypothesis tests. The proportions of correct hypotheses were .45 for PPPP, .52 for PPPN, .41 for PPNN, .35 for PNNN, .16 for NNNN, and .52 for Control. Groups that were instructed to use positive tests on at least two arrays (PPPP, PPPN, and PPNN) and the control condition had a higher proportion of correct hypotheses than the groups that were instructed to use only one positive test or all negative tests.

TABLE 5.3
Mean Proportion of Examples: Experiment 1

	Condition					
	Cont	*PPPP*	*PPPN*	*PPNN*	*PNNN*	*NNNN*
Array 1	$.65_{bc}$	$.71_{ab}$	$.74_a$	$.62_c$	$.57_c$	.45
Array 2	$.65_b$	$.75_a$	$.75_a$	$.64_b$	.28	.45
Array 3	$.68_a$	$.74_a$	$.75_a$	.17	.29	.46
Array 4	$.67_a$	$.70_a$	$.19_{bc}$	$.13_c$	$.26_b$	.43

Note: Within a row means not sharing the same subscript differ significantly.
Source: Laughlin et al. 1997.

In further assessments of positive and negative tests, Laughlin, Shupe, and Magley (1998) considered the transition probabilities from an incorrect hypothesis on trial t to the correct hypothesis on trial $t + 1$ for positive and negative tests followed by examples and nonexamples. These transition probabilities were higher for positive tests than for negative tests, higher for positive tests followed by examples than positive tests followed by nonexamples, and higher for negative tests followed by examples than negative tests followed by nonexamples. Thus positive hypothesis tests are more likely than negative hypothesis tests to be followed by further examples from which the correct rule becomes more apparent.

SIMULTANEOUS COLLECTIVE AND INDIVIDUAL INDUCTION

Consider a research team of virologists and a single virologist who conduct a series of experiments while exchanging predictions (hypotheses) and data (evidence) during each successive experiment. This is an example of *simultaneous collective and individual induction.* We have seen that collective induction is superior to individual induction. In these experiments the groups and individuals solved the problem separately, with no communication between them. Laughlin and McGlynn (1986) conducted an experiment on simultaneous collective and individual induction in which four-person groups and individuals solved the same problem in separate rooms at the same pace. On each trial they exchanged both hypotheses and card plays, hypotheses only, card plays only, or made no exchange. Using an upper case H for exchange of hypotheses and a lower case h for no exchange, and an upper case C for exchange of card plays and a lower case c for no exchange, the four conditions may be abbreviated HC, Hc, hC, and hc.

After being instructed together the group and individual in the HC condition went to separate rooms where the problem began from two cards with the same known positive example (e.g., 8S), one for the group array and one for the individual array. After the group and individual had decided on their first hypotheses, they wrote them on both their hypothesis sheets and index cards. Then the experimenter brought the index card with the group hypothesis to the individual and the index card with the individual hypothesis to the group. Hence the groups knew both their own hypothesis and the individual hypothesis before making their first card play, and the individuals knew both their own hypothesis and the group hypothesis before making their first card play. The experimenter then added the same card that the group chose to the individual array

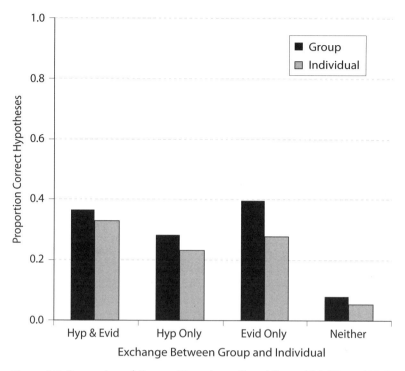

Figure 5.8. Proportion of Correct Hypotheses (Laughlin and McGlynn 1986)

and the same card that the individual chose to the group array. This procedure continued for ten trials, after which the group and individual made their final hypothesis. In the Hc condition they exchanged hypotheses only, in the hC condition they exchanged cards only, and in the hc condition they solved the problem independently without exchange of hypotheses or card plays.

Figure 5.8 gives the proportion of correct hypotheses for the groups and individuals in each of the four exchange conditions. Both the main effect of exchange of hypotheses and the main effect of exchange of evidence were significant, indicating that performance was increased by both exchange of hypotheses and exchange of evidence (card plays). However, a significant three-way interaction indicated that group performance was improved relatively more by exchange of evidence than by exchange of hypotheses.

In a similar experiment (Laughlin 1992) a four-person group and four separate individuals exchanged both hypotheses and evidence (card choices) on each trial, exchanged hypotheses but not evidence, exchanged evidence but not hypotheses, or solved the problem independently with

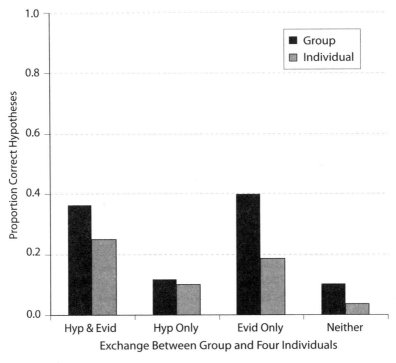

Figure 5.9. Proportion of Correct Hypotheses (Laughlin 1992)

no exchange. The four individuals made no exchange with one another. Figure 5.9 gives the proportion of correct hypotheses for groups and individuals in the four conditions. Group performance was improved by exchange of evidence but not by exchange of hypotheses.

These results demonstrate the value of further evidence from other individuals in improving performance in collective induction. Just as performance improved with increasing arrays of evidence selected by the group (Laughlin, VanderStoep, and Hollingshead 1991), performance also improved with increasing arrays of evidence selected by other individuals. In contrast, additional hypotheses from other individuals had less effect, just as multiple hypotheses did not increase the number of correct hypotheses in the experiment of Laughlin, Bonner, and Altermatt (1998). The groups profited from further evidence but not from further hypotheses.

These two experiments also assessed group influence on the individual and individual influence on the group. Let the single correct hypothesis be C, different plausible hypotheses be A, B, D, and E, and different nonplausible hypotheses be F, G, H, and I. On each trial t and subsequent

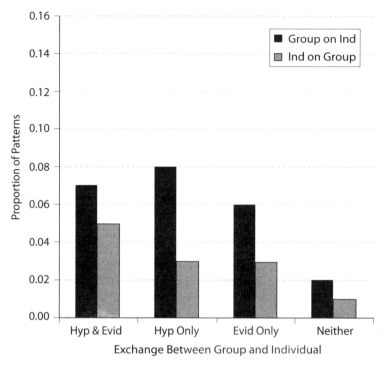

Figure 5.10. Influence of Group on Individual and Individual on Group (Laughlin and McGlynn 1986)

trial t + 1 the individual and the group propose a hypothesis. Represent these four hypotheses by a pattern of four left-to-right letters: the first letter is the individual hypothesis on trial t, the second letter is the individual hypothesis on trial t + 1, the third letter is the group hypothesis on trial t, and the fourth letter is the group hypothesis on trial t + 1. Code the plausible hypotheses in the order A, B, D, E as necessary and reset them in this order for each new trial t. Likewise, code the nonplausible hypotheses in the order F, G, H, I as necessary and reset them in this order for each new trial t (Laughlin 1992, p. 451).

For example, the CCAC pattern indicates the influence of a correct individual on the group, and the ACCC pattern indicates the influence of a correct group on the individual. As indicated in Figures 5.10 and 5.11, there was more influence of the group on the individuals than the individuals on the group. In addition to being effective problem-solving systems, cooperative groups may effectively influence individuals who are apart from the group but working on the same problem.

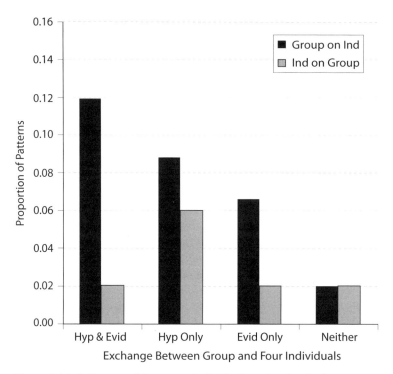

Figure 5.11. Influence of Group on Individuals and Individuals on Group (Laughlin 1992)

SOCIAL COMBINATION PROCESSES

Denote the correct hypothesis as C, plausible hypotheses as P, and non-plausible hypotheses as N, following each C, P, or N by the number of group members (1 to 4) who propose it. For example, C3P1 indicates that three members propose the correct hypothesis and one member proposes a plausible hypothesis. C1P2P1 indicates that one member proposes the correct hypothesis, two members propose the same plausible hypothesis, and one member proposes another plausible hypothesis. There are thirty-eight possible distributions of member hypotheses: C4, C3P1, C3N1, . . . , N1N1N1N1. These thirty-eight distributions are the rows of a social combination model. There are eleven possible types of group hypotheses on each trial, the single correct hypothesis, a plausible hypothesis proposed by four, three, two, or one group members, an emergent plausible hypothesis not proposed by any group member (P0), a nonplausible hypothesis proposed by four, three, two, or one group members, or an emergent nonplausible hypothesis not proposed by any group member (N0). These eleven possible types of group hypotheses, C, P4, P3, P2, P1, P0, N4, N3, N2, N1, and N0, are the columns of a social combination matrix.

Laughlin, VanderStoep, and Hollingshead (1991) examined the social combination matrix in previous research (Laughlin and McGlynn 1986; Laughlin 1988) and proposed that it could be generated by two postulates:

> *Postulate 1*: If at least two group members propose correct and/or plausible hypotheses, the group selects among those hypotheses only; otherwise, the group selects among all proposed hypotheses.

> *Postulate 2*: If a majority of members propose the same hypothesis, the group follows a majority social combination process; otherwise, the group follows a proportionality process and proposes an emergent hypothesis with probability $1/(H + 1)$, where H is the number of proposed hypotheses (group members).

Table 5.4 gives the predicted probabilities of the eleven types of group hypotheses and group responses for distributions of member hypotheses from Postulates 1 and 2. Table 5.5 gives the results of model testing for Postulates 1 and 2 (POST) and five other plausible models for the aggregate data of 616 four-person groups in seven experiments (Laughlin 1988, 1992; Laughlin, Magley, and Shupe 1997, Laughlin and McGlynn 1986; Laughlin and Shupe 1996; Laughlin, Shupe, and Magley 1998; Laughlin, VanderStoep, and Hollingshead 1991). These five models were: (1) Equiprobability; (2) Majority, Plurality Otherwise, Proportionality Otherwise; (3) Proportionality; (4) Correct-Supported Wins, Majority Otherwise, Plurality Otherwise, Proportionality Otherwise; and (5) Correct Wins, Majority Otherwise, Plurality Otherwise, Proportionality Otherwise.

The predicted proportions of each group hypothesis for each distribution of member hypotheses were determined for each model by multiplying the predicted probabilities of each group hypothesis by the respective row sum and dividing by the total number of group hypotheses. Table 5.5 gives the results of Kolmogorov-Smirnov one-sample tests of the predicted and obtained proportions for each model. Inspection of Table 5.5 indicates lower Dmax values for POST than each of the other models. Using the number of groups (616) the critical value of Dmax at $p > .20$ is .04. The bottom part of Table 5.5 indicates that POST provides an acceptable fit, whereas each of the other five models may be rejected.

In summary, there is a complex but orderly social combination process in collective induction that may be described by Postulates 1 and 2. Postulate 1 specifies the member hypotheses that are considered by the group in proposing a group hypothesis, and Postulate 2 specifies the

TABLE 5.4
Predicted Probabilities of Group Hypotheses for
Distributions of Member Hypotheses

Distribution	Group Hypothesis										
	C	P4	P3	P2	P1	P0	N4	N3	N2	N1	N0
C4	1.00	—	—	—	—	.00	—	—	—	—	.00
C3P1	1.00	—	—	—	.00	.00	—	—	—	—	.00
C3N1	1.00	—	—	—	—	.00	—	—	—	.00	.00
C2P2	.40	—	—	.40	—	.20	—	—	—	—	.00
C2P1P1	.40	—	—	—	.40	.20	—	—	—	—	.00
C2P1N1	.53	—	—	—	.27	.20	—	—	—	.00	.00
C2N2	.80	—	—	—	—	.20	—	—	.00	.00	.00
C2N1N1	.80	—	—	—	—	.20	—	—	—	.00	.00
C1P3	.00	—	1.00	—	—	.00	—	—	—	—	.00
C1P2P1	.20	—	—	.40	.20	.20	—	—	—	—	.00
C1P2N1	.27	—	—	.53	—	.20	—	—	—	.00	.00
C1P1P1P1	.20	—	—	—	.60	.20	—	—	—	—	.00
C1P1P1N1	.27	—	—	—	.53	.20	—	—	—	.00	.00
C1P1N2	.40	—	—	—	.40	.20	—	—	.00	—	.00
C1P1N1N1	.40	—	—	—	.40	.20	—	—	—	.00	.00
C1N3	.00	—	—	—	—	.00	—	1.00	—	—	.00
C1N2N1	.20	—	—	—	—	.05	—	—	.40	.20	.15
C1N1N1N1	.20	—	—	—	—	.05	—	—	—	.60	.15
P4	.00	1.00	—	—	—	.00	—	—	—	—	.00
P3P1	.00	—	1.00	—	.00	.00	—	—	—	—	.00
P3N1	.00	—	1.00	—	—	.00	—	—	—	.00	.00
P2P2	.00	—	—	.80	—	.20	—	—	—	—	.00
P2P1P1	.00	—	—	.40	.40	.20	—	—	—	—	.00
P2P1N1	.00	—	—	.53	.27	.20	—	—	—	.00	.00
P2N2	.00	—	—	.80	—	.20	—	—	.00	—	.00
P2N1N1	.00	—	—	.80	—	.20	—	—	—	.00	.00
P1P1P1P1	.00	—	—	—	.80	.20	—	—	—	—	.00
P1P1P1N1	.00	—	—	—	.80	.20	—	—	—	.00	.00
P1P1N2	.00	—	—	—	.80	.20	—	—	.00	—	.00
P1P1N1N1	.00	—	—	—	.80	.20	—	—	—	.00	.00
P1N3	.00	—	—	—	.00	.00	—	1.00	—	—	.00
P1N2N1	.00	—	—	—	.20	.05	—	—	.40	.20	.15
P1N1N1N1	.00	—	—	—	.20	.05	—	—	—	.60	.15
N4	.00	—	—	—	—	.00	1.00	—	—	—	.00
N3N1	.00	—	—	—	—	.00	—	1.00	—	—	.00
N2N2	.00	—	—	—	—	.00	—	—	.80	—	.20
N2N1N1	.00	—	—	—	—	.00	—	—	.40	.40	.20
N1N1N1N1	.00	—	—	—	—	.00	—	—	—	.80	.20

Source: Laughlin 1999.

TABLE 5.5

Obtained Probabilities of Group Hypotheses for Distributions
of Member Hypotheses for 616 Four-Person Groups

| | Group Hypothesis | | | | | | | | | | | |
Distribution	C	P4	P3	P2	P1	P0	N4	N3	N2	N1	N0	Sum
C4	1.00	—	—	—	—	.00	—	—	—	—	.00	1,854
C3P1	.90	—	—	—	.06	.04	—	—	—	—	.01	363
C3N1	.90	—	—	—	—	.03	—	—	—	.06	.01	118
C2P2	.51	—	—	.44	—	.03	—	—	—	—	.02	93
C2P1P1	.65	—	—	—	.23	.11	—	—	—	—	.01	140
C2P1N1	.67	—	—	—	.16	.12	—	—	—	.04	.02	57
C2N2	.00	—	—	—	—	1.00	—	—	.00	—	.00	4
C2N1N1	.80	—	—	—	—	.00	—	—	—	.20	.00	15
C1P3	.17	—	.80	—	—	.03	—	—	—	—	.00	95
C1P2P1	.24	—	—	.57	.07	.12	—	—	—	—	.00	112
C1P2N1	.26	—	—	.64	—	.07	—	—	—	.00	.02	42
C1P1P1P1	.41	—	—	—	.30	.26	—	—	—	—	.03	147
C1P1P1N1	.29	—	—	—	.40	.23	—	—	—	.05	.04	83
C1P1N2	.00	—	—	—	.20	.20	—	—	.40	—	.20	5
C1P1N1N1	.47	—	—	—	.16	.25	—	—	—	.03	.09	32
C1N3	.00	—	—	—	—	.00	—	1.00	—	—	.00	1
C1N2N1	.00	—	—	—	—	.00	—	—	.75	.25	.00	4
C1N1N1N1	.67	—	—	—	—	.11	—	—	—	.11	.11	9
P4	.00	.97	—	—	—	.02	—	—	—	—	.00	1,498
P3P1	.00	—	.87	—	.08	.04	—	—	—	—	.01	1,202
P3N1	.01	—	.90	—	—	.03	—	—	—	.05	.02	288
P2P2	.01	—	—	.93	—	.06	—	—	—	—	.01	325
P2P1P1	.01	—	—	.61	.26	.11	—	—	—	—	.01	1,128
P2P1N1	.01	—	—	.62	.17	.12	—	—	—	.06	.03	411
P2N2	.00	—	—	.58	—	.08	—	—	.32	—	.02	53
P2N1N1	.00	—	—	.67	—	.12	—	—	—	.13	.07	67
P1P1P1P1	.01	—	—	—	.71	.25	—	—	—	—	.02	715
P1P1P1N1	.03	—	—	—	.62	.24	—	—	—	.04	.06	464
P1P1N2	.00	—	—	—	.47	.12	—	—	.38	—	.02	81
P1P1N1N1	.03	—	—	—	.43	.25	—	—	—	.18	.12	284
P1N3	.00	—	—	—	.13	.06	—	.81	—	—	.00	54
P1N2N1	.04	—	—	—	.25	.12	—	—	.44	.06	.09	68
P1N1N1N1	.04	—	—	—	.38	.20	—	—	—	.24	.14	138
N4	.02	—	—	—	—	.00	.97	—	—	—	.01	60
N3N1	.14	—	—	—	—	.00	—	.79	—	.07	.00	28
N2N2	.00	—	—	—	—	.00	—	—	1.00	—	.00	6
N2N1N1	.00	—	—	—	—	.10	—	—	.77	.10	.03	31
N1N1N1N1	.00	—	—	—	—	.26	—	—	—	.31	.43	74
Proportion	.26	.14	.14	.14	.16	.09	.01	.00	.01	.02	.02	
Predicted by POST	.25	.15	.16	.11	.21	.09	.01	.01	.01	.02	.01	
$\overline{D}$ POST	.01	.01	.01	.02	.02	.02	.02	.02	.02	.02	.00	
$\overline{D}$ EQUI	.02	.01	.07	.12	.03	.05	.05	.05	.05	.02	.00	
$\overline{D}$ MPP	.00	.00	.02	.09	.07	.02	.02	.02	.01	.02	.00	
$\overline{D}$ PROP	.02	.01	.03	.05	.05	.04	.04	.04	.04	.02	.00	
$\overline{D}$ CSW	.00	.00	.03	.09	.07	.02	.02	.01	.01	.02	.00	
$\overline{\underline{D}}$ CW	.05	.05	.06	.11	.07	.01	.01	.01	.00	.02	.00	

Source: Laughlin 1999.

social combination process by which the groups map the distribution of member hypotheses to a group hypothesis.

A Theory of Collective Induction

Table 5.6 presents a theory of collective induction in the form of twelve postulates that summarize this research program (Laughlin and Hollingshead 1995; Laughlin 1996, 1999). Postulates 1 through 5 set collective induction within a general theory of group problem solving and decision making. Postulate 6 specifies the nature of induction and Postulates 7 and 8 (corresponding to Postulates 1 and 2 in the previous section of this chapter) formalize the social combination process in collective induction. Postulates 9 through 12 formalize research on collective induction versus individual induction, the relative value of multiple hypotheses and multiple evidence in collective induction, simultaneous collective and individual induction, and positive and negative hypothesis tests in collective induction, as presented in the previous sections of this chapter.

In conclusion, the twelve postulates organize a large amount of previous theory and research on group decision making in general (Postulates 1–5) and collective induction in rule learning in particular (Postulates 6–12). The rule induction task abstracts the essential features of collective

TABLE 5.6
Collective Induction: Twelve Postulates

Postulate 1: Cooperative decision-making groups may resolve disagreement among their members in formulating a collective group response in five ways:
1. Random selection among proposed alternatives.
2. Voting among proposed alternatives.
3. Turntaking among proposed alternatives.
4. Demonstration of preferability of a proposed alternative.
5. Generation of a new emergent alternative.

Postulate 2: The five ways of resolving disagreement may be formalized by social combination models:
1. Random selection: equiprobability model.
2. Voting: majority and plurality models.
3. Turntaking: proportionality model.
4. Demonstration: truth-wins and truth-supported wins models.
5. Generation of a new emergent alternative: specified probability of an alternative not proposed by any member.

---

continued on next page

TABLE 5.6 *(continued)*
Collective Induction: Twelve Postulates

Postulate 3: Cooperative group tasks may be ordered on a continuum anchored by intellective and judgmental tasks. Intellective tasks are problems or decisions for which there is a demonstrably correct response (e.g., algebra problems). Judgmental tasks are evaluative, behavioral, or aesthetic judgments for which there is no demonstrably correct response (e.g., jury decisions).

Postulate 4: A demonstrably correct response requires four conditions:
1. Group consensus on a conceptual system.
2. Sufficient information.
3. Incorrect members are able to recognize the correct response if it is proposed.
4. Correct members have sufficient ability, motivation, and time to demonstrate the correct response to the incorrect members.

Postulate 5: The proportion of group members that is necessary and sufficient for a collective decision is inversely proportional to the demonstrability of the proposed group response.

Postulate 6: Inductive tasks are both intellective and judgmental: nonplausible hypotheses may be demonstrated to be nonplausible (intellective), but correct hypotheses may not be demonstrated to be uniquely correct relative to other plausible hypotheses that also fit the evidence (judgmental).

Postulate 7: If at least two group members propose correct and/or plausible hypotheses, the group selects among those hypotheses only (demonstration); otherwise, the group selects among all proposed hypotheses.

Postulate 8: If a majority of members propose the same hypothesis, the group follows a majority social combination process (voting); otherwise, the group follows a proportionality process (turntaking) and proposes an emergent hypothesis with probability $1/(H + 1)$, where H is the number of proposed hypotheses (group members).

Postulate 9: Given sufficient information and time, collective induction is comparable to the induction of the best of an equivalent number of independent individuals.

Postulate 10: Collective induction is improved more by multiple evidence than by multiple hypotheses.

Postulate 11: There is more group influence on individuals than individual influence on groups in simultaneous collective and individual induction.

Postulate 12: Positive hypothesis tests are generally more effective than negative hypothesis tests in collective induction.

Source: Laughlin 1999.

induction: each hypothesis corresponds to a proposed generalization, and each card play corresponds to an experiment designed to assess the generalization by a positive or negative test. The set of possible hypotheses is indeterminate at the outset of the problem, corresponding to the large number of initially indeterminate possible hypotheses in a real-world inductive domain. The progressive array of example and nonexample cards corresponds to the progressive growth of evidence and the concomitant reduction in the number of possible hypotheses with ongoing research in a real-world inductive domain. Postulates 9 through 12 summarize the orderly results of research on group versus individual induction, the relative effects of multiple hypotheses and multiple evidence, group and individual influence in simultaneous collective and individual induction, and the relative effectiveness of positive hypothesis tests and negative hypothesis tests. Because of these abstractions of the essential features of collective induction, the theory should have implications for the cooperative groups and teams such as scientific research teams, auditors, financial analysts, art experts, and other groups and teams who seek collective inductions in many domains.

Collective Induction in Competitive Auctions

In an insightful and creative study Maciejovsky and Budescu (2007, pp. 8–9) noted that competitive auctions, where participants bid (typically in money) on goods without communication, fulfill several of the postulates of the theory of collective induction (Laughlin 1999).

> Despite the obvious difference between their cooperative and competitive aspects, groups and auctions share a number of important features. This becomes apparent upon examination of the theoretical framework of collective induction encapsulated in Laughlin's 12 postulates (Laughlin 1999). Postulates 3 and 5, taken jointly, imply that groups can solve intellective tasks correctly, even if only a small minority of participants (as small as a single person for mathematical problems) knows the correct solution. Postulate 9 states that collective induction is comparable in quality to the best solution proposed by (a similar number of) individuals. Finally, Postulate 4 lists the four conditions required for demonstrability. The first two refer to the group and the decision environment: (a) the group should agree on a conceptual system (rules, terminology, etc.), and (b) there should be sufficient information available for the group to find a solution. The other two conditions refer to individual participants: (c) members who endorse incorrect solutions should be able to recognize the correct solution if it is presented to them, and (d) members who know the correct solution should

have the ability, time, and motivation to demonstrate it to those who hold incorrect beliefs. Clearly, the motivation to cooperate with other members is a critical component of this process.

Maciejovsky and Budescu (2007, p. 9) then note the corresponding features of competitive auctions in effectively disseminating and integrating information without the cooperation in face-to-face groups:

> The corresponding features of competitive auctions relate to their ability to disseminate and aggregate information effectively. Analyses of aggregate market variables, such as prices, reflect the solution to a problem, even if only a small minority of traders solved it individually, implying that Postulates 3, 5, and 9 are satisfied. Markets also satisfy most conditions of Postulate 4: (a) Auctions apply strict and commonly known rules (e.g., how and when to submit bids, how to determine auction winners); (b) traders have the necessary information to identify the correct solution to a task; and (c) auction participants who endorse incorrect solutions are able to recognize the correct solution when exposed to a variety of structured information (e.g., who bids, how much, on what), which is public knowledge. The key difference between interactive groups and auctions pertains to the last condition: (d) Auction participants who know the correct solution (i.e., the value of the good) do not necessarily want to share their information with others. In fact, they have strong incentives not to divulge it to their competitors, but the public nature of the auction prevents them from withholding it indefinitely (although they could adopt various convoluted strategies designed to disguise it at least temporarily). The main goal of this study is to compare these two institutions.

Maciejovsky and Budescu (2007) used the Wason (1966) four-card task. There are four cards with the letters A or D on one side and the numbers 4 or 7 on the other side:

Card	Side One	Side Two
One	A	4
Two	A	7
Three	D	4
Four	D	7

The four cards are placed on a table. The visible (up) sides of the four cards are:

A   D   4   7

The problem is: Which are the minimum cards that need to be turned over to verify the rule "If there is a vowel on one side of the card, then there is an even number on the other side?"

In formal logic this is an example of the logical relation of implication: if p, then q, or p implies q. The truth table for implication is:

		p implies q
p	q	true
p	not q	false
not p	q	true
not p	not q	true

Here:

A	4	true
A	7	false
D	4	true
D	7	true

Thus to verify the rule only the A card (p) and the 7 card (not q) need to be turned over. The A card is turned over to see if there is a 4 on the other side, and the 7 card is turned over to see if there is an A on the other side. Virtually everybody realizes that the A card must be turned over to verify the rule, but few people realize that the 7 card must be turned over to falsify the rule.

Study 1 of Maciejovsky and Budescu (2007) involved three stages. In Stage 1 the participants solved an implication problem individually but were not given feedback as to whether they were correct. In Stage 2 they solved a new implication problem in a cooperative group. In Stage 3 they solved one or eight implication problems as individuals.

Only 9% of the participants chose the two correct cards (p and not q) in Stage 1, and 50% of the groups chose the two correct cards in Stage 2, a dramatic improvement. All six groups with at least one member who had solved the problem correctly solved the new problem (truth wins), and four of the fourteen groups without a member who had solved the problem correctly solved the problem. Stage 3 assesses group-to-individual transfer, which we consider in chapter 7.

Study 2 of Maciejovsky and Budescu (2007) again had three stages. As in Study 1, individuals solved implication problems in Stages 1 and 3.

The percentage of correct solutions in Stage 1 was 13%, which is similar to Study 1 and justifies a comparison of Stage 2 in the two studies.

In Stage 2 of Study 2 four participants engaged in a competitive auction with payoff feedback. They were given an implication rule and told that the objective was to acquire the minimum number of cards that they thought satisfied the correct rule by bidding for any of the fifteen combinations of cards (Card 1, Card 2, Card 3, Card 4, Cards 1 and 2, . . . , Cards 1, 2, 3, and 4). At the beginning of each of thirty one-minute trials each of the four participants was endowed with 500 Experimental

Credit Units (ECU), and bid any number of them on any combination of cards (say, 100 ECU for the bundle of Cards 1 and 3). Each set of acquired cards that satisfied the correct solution (i.e., the p and not q cards) earned a dividend of 200 ECU. To increase competition, the Auctioneer (a computer program) auctioned off only four cards of each type on each trial, distributing the cards to different bidders in a way to maximize the Auctioneer's profit. The remaining unbid ECU did not carry over trials ("bid it or lose it"). Bids were entered and feedback given at a computer terminal for each participant.

Two feedback conditions were presented on the terminal screen. In the Private Feedback Condition participants were told only about the outcome of their own bids. If their bids were successful, they received full information about their dividends and their net rewards (dividends minus bids) at the end of each of the thirty trials. In the Public Feedback Condition each participant received this information for all four participants.

Correct responses were defined as identification of the correct solution by the end of the auction by analysis of the bids. The correct solution was identified in $10/12 = 83\%$ of the auctions with public feedback and $11/20 = 55\%$ of the auctions with private feedback. Thus the participants in the competitive auction were as successful in identifying the correct rule as the participants in the cooperative face-to-face groups.

In Study 3 of Maciejovsky and Budescu (2007) there were again three stages. As in Study 1, individuals solved implication problems in Stages 1 and 3.

The percentage of correct solutions in Stage 1 was 13%. In Stage 2 four participants engaged in a competitive auction similar to that of Study 2, but without feedback. In another change from Study 2, participants who correctly solved the problem alone in Stage 1 were defined as "insiders," and 0, 1, or 2 insiders were assigned to different auctions. The correct solution was not identified in any of the eight auctions without an insider. The correct solution was identified in $2/8 = 25\%$ of the auctions with one insider and $11/32 = 34\%$ of the auctions with two insiders. This indicates the spread of influence from one or two correct participants through their bids in the competitive auction.

Maciejovsky and Budescu (2007, p. 33) propose that a key feature of interacting cooperative groups and competitive auctions is that both provide an opportunity to develop a shared mental model of the problem.

We argued that despite the difference between the groups' *cooperative* nature and the auctions' *competitive* nature, auctions meet four of the postulates stipulated for collective induction in groups (Laughlin 1999): a conceptual system with known rules and terminology (4a), sufficient information (4b), ability to recognize the solution to a problem (4c), incentives for correct solutions (3 and 5), and aggregate solutions comparable in quality to the best (of a similar number) of individuals (9).

In summary, participants in a competitive auction without interaction were as successful in solving the implication problems as participants in an interacting face-to-face cooperative problem-solving group because both information exchange and integration procedures enable the participants to develop a shared mental model of the problem.

Chapter Six

LETTERS-TO-NUMBERS PROBLEMS

IN CHAPTER 5 we have seen that, given sufficient information and time, groups perform *as well as* the best of an equivalent number of individuals on rule induction problems. We now report research on highly intellective letters-to-numbers coding problems on which groups perform *better than* the best of an equivalent number of individuals. We first explain letters-to-numbers problems and present the instructions to the problem-solving group or individual. We then consider several possible strategies of increasing effectiveness. Next we report the results of three experiments comparing groups and the best of an equivalent number of individuals.

LETTERS-TO-NUMBERS PROBLEMS

In letters-to-numbers problems the ten letters *A, B, C, D, E, F, G, H, I,* and *J* are randomly coded to the ten numbers 0, 1, 2, 3, 4, 5, 6, 7, 8, and 9. The objective is to figure out the coding in as few trials as possible. The instructions for groups are the following:

> This is an experiment in problem solving. The objective is to figure out a code in as few trials as possible. The numbers 0–9 have been coded as the letters *A–J* in some random order. You will be trying to find out which letter corresponds to which number. It is important to remember that all we are doing is changing the characters used to represent the numbers. We are not changing the way that the number system works. That is, we are still using the same decimal number system you have been using all of your life. Below is an example of a random code:
>
> $A = 3, B = 5, C = 8, D = 2, E = 1, F = 6, G = 4, H = 7, I = 0, J = 9$
>
> First you will come up with an addition or subtraction equation using the letters *A* to *J* that will be solved by the experimenter who will give you the answer in letter form. Then you will make a guess as to what one of the letters represents, and we will tell you whether or not the guess is correct. Then you will propose the full mapping of the ten letters to the ten numbers. When you have proposed the full correct mapping of the ten letters to the ten numbers you will have solved the problem. The objective is to solve the

problem in as few trials as possible. Here are four example trials using the random code above. Note that underlined letters represent experimenter feedback.

Trial	Equation	Hypothesis	Feedback
1	$A + B = \underline{C}$	$A = 1$	False
2	$B + C = \underline{EA}$	$A = 8$	False
3	$F + A + D = \underline{EE}$	$E = 1$	True
4	$H - J = \underline{-D}$	$I = 0$	True

On the first trial the person chooses the equation $A + B = ?$ and the experimenter tells the person that the solution to this equation is C. This is because $A = 3$ and $B = 5$, which sums to 8, the letter represented by C. The person then guesses that A represents the number 1 and the experimenter indicates that this is not the case, or False. On the second trial the person asks the solution to the equation $B + C = ?$ and is told that the answer is EA. This is because $B = 5$ and $C=8$, which sums to 13 or EA. Note that on the third trial the person chooses to add three letters together. You may use as many letters as you desire in your equations. Note that on the fourth trial the person chooses to use a subtraction equation. You may use either addition or subtraction equations as you see fit.

In the group condition each group member has a response sheet. On each trial the group discusses, until consensus is reached, a proposed equation (e.g., $A + D = ?$), which each member writes on their response sheet. The experimenter then solves the equation and gives the answer in letters (e.g., $A + D = B$) and each group member writes the answer on their response sheet. The group then proposes a hypothesis for the coding of one letter (e.g., $A = 6$). The experimenter then states whether or not the group hypothesis is correct, and each member circles Y (for Yes, it is correct) or N (for No, it is not correct) on a column on their response sheet. The group then discusses and fills out a proposed full coding of the ten letters to the ten numbers (e.g., $A = 4$, $B = 9$, $J = 7$, etc.), which all members write on their response sheet. The experimenter then checks the coding of the ten letters to numbers and states whether or not it is completely correct. The full correct group coding solves the problem, whereas an incorrect coding requires another trial, up to a maximum of ten trials. All group members have scratch paper for notes.

Letters-to-Numbers Strategies

Correct codings of letters to numbers may be conclusively demonstrated in at least three ways. First, the experimenter gives feedback on a proposed hypothesis on each trial (e.g., True, A is 3). Second, correct codings may be demonstrated by arithmetic and algebra (e.g., if A is known to be 3 and B is known to be 5, the answer to the proposed equation $A + B = C$ identifies C as 8). Third, correct codings may be demonstrated by logic (e.g., if $F + G = EI$, E must be 1). Moreover, codings may be demonstrated to be plausible or nonplausible by transitivity and the other properties of the ordinary number system (e.g., if $A + B = C$, C must be greater than both A and B). Conversely, proposed codings may be demonstrated to be erroneous by their inconsistency with experimenter feedback, arithmetic, algebra, logic, or the properties of the ordinary number system. Here let us consider possible strategies on letters-to-numbers problems.

Two-Letter Substitution Strategy

After identifying one letter, the problems may be solved by a series of proposed two-letter equations:

Trial	Equation	Hypothesis	Feedback
1	$A + J = ED$	$E = 1$	True
2	$E + E = D$	$D = 2$	True
3	$D + D = G$	$G = 4$	True
4	$E + D = A$	$A = 3$	True
5	$A + G = H$	$H = 7$	True
6	$D + H = J$	$J = 9$	True
7	$A + D = B$	$B = 5$	True
8	$A + A = F$	$F = 6$	True
9	$G + G = C$	$C = 8$	True

Note: $A = 3$, $B = 5$, $C = 8$, $D = 2$, $E = 1$, $F = 6$, $G = 4$, $H = 7$, $I = 0$, $J = 9$

After feedback on Trial 9, nine of the letters have been identified, and the remaining letter I which is coded as 0 follows by exclusion. Hence the problem is solved in nine trials.

Although such a two-letter substitution strategy will solve the problem in the allowed maximum of ten trials, it is obviously suboptimal. The hypotheses inefficiently test what is already known from the answers to the proposed equations. There are no further inferences beyond the simple substitutions. For example, the identification of E as 1 on Trial 1, D as 2 on Trial 2, and A as 3 on Trial 4 implies that J is 9 on Trial 1.

Multiletter Substitution Strategy

Equations with more than two letters will generally provide more information than will equations with only two letters. For example, consider the first two trials of the previous illustration of a two-letter substitution strategy. After the *E* is identified as 1 on Trial 1 and the *D* is identified as 2 on Trial 2, the proposed equation and answer *ED + DD = AG* on Trial 3 would identify the *A* as 3 and the *G* as 4. Similarly, the more complex equation and answer *EEE + EED + EDD + DDD = BFH* on Trial 3 would identify the *B* as 5, *F* as 6, and *H* as 7. This illustrates the general principle that as the number of letters per equation increases the equation will identify increasingly more letters.

Trial	Equation	Hypothesis	Feedback
1	$A + J = ED$	$B = 0$	False
2	$E + E = D$	$C = 0$	False
3	$EEE + EED + EDD = AGB$	$F = 0$	False
4	$DDDA + DDAA + DAAA = FHCJ$	$I = 0$	True

Note: A = 3, B = 5, C = 8, D = 2, E = 1, F = 6, G = 4, H = 7, I = 0, J = 9

Known Answer Strategy

In a substitution strategy of any degree of complexity, the known letters are proposed on the left side of the equation in order to identify the unknown letters on the right side of the equation. Another strategy uses the anticipated answer on the right side of the proposed equation to identify letters on the left side of the equation. To illustrate, consider the following strategy, again assuming the same correct coding:

Trial	Equation	Hypothesis	Feedback
1	$A + B + C + D + E + F + G + H + I + J = GB$	$A = 7$	False
2	$A + C + D + E + F + H + I + J = AF$	$D = 3$	False
3.	$C + D + E + H + I + J = DH$	$C = 0$	False
4	$C + E + I + J = EC$	$I = 9$	False

Note: A = 3, B = 5, C = 8, D = 2, E = 1, F = 6, G = 4, H = 7, I = 0, J = 9

The sum of the integers from 1 to *N* is given by the formula $N(N + 1)/2$. Hence the answer to the equation that adds all ten letters—$A + B + C + D + E + F + G + H + I + J = ?$—will be $9(10)/2 = 45$, as the letter coded as 0 will have no effect. Equation 1 adds all ten letters, identifying *G* as 4 and *B* as 5. Adding the remaining eight letters in Equation 2 has a known answer of 36, identifying the *A* as 3 and *F* as 6. Adding the remaining six letters in Equation 3 has a known answer of 27, identifying the *D* as 2 and *H* as 7. Similarly, adding the remaining four letters in Equation 4 has a known answer of 18, identifying the *E* as 1 and the *C* as 8. At this point the two letters *I* and *J* remain to be coded to the numbers 0 and 9. The hypothesis on Trial 4 tests $I = 9$ and the feedback False identifies the *I* as 0 and *J* as 9. Equations 1 through 4 exemplify a known answer strategy (Laughlin, Bonner, and Miner 2002) in which the known answer on the right side of the equation identifies letters on the left side, in contrast to a substitution strategy where the known letters on the left side of the equation are used to identify unknown letters on the right side.

Combined Known Answer and Multiletter Substitution Strategy

A combined strategy again begins by adding all ten letters, with the answer known in advance to be $9(10)/2 = 45$, identifying G as 4 and B as 5. The letter G is then used in the multiletter Equation 2 to identify E as 1, A as 3, and D as 2. The letters E, D, A, G, and B are then used in the multiletter Equation 3 to identify F as 6, H as 7, C as 8, and J as 9. The remaining letter I is known by exclusion, solving in three trials.

Trial	Equation	Hypothesis	Feedback
1	$A + B + C + D + E + F + G + H + I + J = GB$	$A = 0$	False
2	$GG + GG + GG = EAD$	$C = 0$	False
3	$EDAG + BBBB = FHCJ$	$I = 0$	True

Note: $A = 3, B = 5, C = 8, D = 2, E = 1, F = 6, G = 4, H = 7, I = 0, J = 9$

These illustrations indicate that letters-to-numbers problems may be solved by a variety of increasingly effective strategies. We now present three experiments that compared groups and the best of an equivalent number of individuals on letters-to-numbers problems. Because the problems are highly intellective the authors expected that the groups would solve the problems in fewer trials than the best individuals and use more effective strategies.

Groups Perform Better Than the Best Individuals

In an experiment by Laughlin, Bonner, and Miner (2002) 328 participants solved a letters-to-numbers problem as a four-person cooperative group, and 328 did so as individuals. The experiment was run as a randomized blocks design with a group of four and four individuals assigned to one of twenty-four codings of letters to numbers in succession. The instructions and procedures were as given previously. The best, second-best, third-best, and fourth-best individuals were defined by the number of trials to solution for each set of four individuals for each replication (nonsolvers in the allotted ten trials were considered to require eleven trials).

Trials to Solution

Figure 6.1 gives the mean trials to solution for the groups and first, second, third, and fourth individuals. All the pairwise comparisons of the

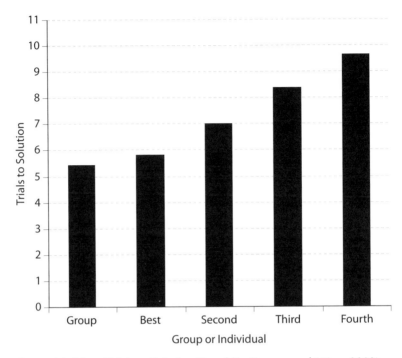

Figure 6.1. Mean Trials to Solution (Laughlin, Bonner, and Miner 2002)

five means were significant. Thus the groups performed better than the best individuals on the basic criterion of trials to solution.

Letters per Equation

Figure 6.2 gives the mean letters per equation. As indicated in Figure 6.2, the groups proposed more complex equations than each of the best, second-best, third-best, and fourth-best individuals.

Letters Identified per Equation

The protocols were scored for the trial on which a given letter was identified by experimenter feedback that a proposed hypothesis (e.g., $A = 3$) was True, numerical and logical inference, or exclusion when only one unidentified letter remained. Figure 6.3 gives the mean letters identified per equation. The total number of letters identified (0–10) was divided by the number of trials to give the letters identified per equation. As

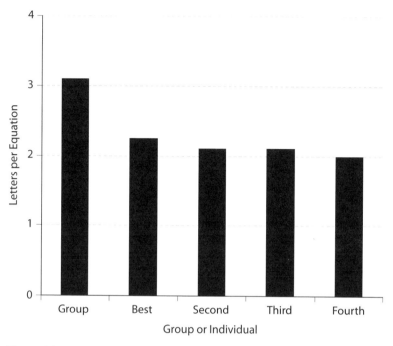

Figure 6.2. Mean Letters per Equation (Laughlin, Bonner, and Miner 2002)

indicated in Figure 6.3, the groups identified more letters per equation than the best individuals.

Two-Letter Substitution Strategy

In a two-letter substitution strategy all proposed equations either add two letters (e.g. $A + B = ?$) or subtract one letter from another (e.g., $A - B = ?$). A two-letter substitution strategy was used exclusively by 49% of the groups, 65% of the best individuals, 72% of the second-best individuals, 77% of the third-best individuals, and 71% of the fourth-best individuals, a significantly lower proportion of two-letter substitution strategies for the groups than the best individuals.

Known Answer Strategy

Sixteen of the groups, five of the best individuals, one of the second-best individuals, one of the third-best individuals, and none of the fourth-best

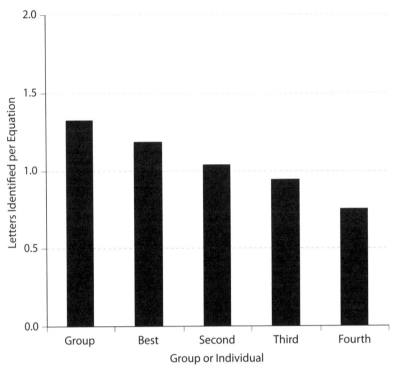

Figure 6.3. Mean Letters Identified per Equation (Laughlin, Bonner, and Miner 2002)

individuals proposed the known answer equation that added all ten letters, thus identifying the letters coded as 4 and 5. The groups had a higher proportion of these equations (16/82 = .195) than the best individuals (5/82 = .061) and all individuals combined.

Summary of Results

The four-person groups had significantly fewer trials to solution than each of the best, second-best, third-best, and fourth-best of an equivalent number of individuals. The groups had fewer trials to solution, proposed more letters per equation, identified more letters per equation, used fewer inefficient two-letter substitution strategies, and proposed more known answer equations than each of the best, second-best, third-best, and fourth-best individuals. Extending the large amount of research over seven decades that had supported the robust generalization that cooperative groups perform better than the *average* individual in problem solving (recall the references in chapter 2) this experiment was the first reported evidence that cooperative problem-solving groups perform better than the *best* of an equivalent number of independent individuals.

Discussion

Letters-to-numbers problems strongly fulfill the four conditions of demonstrability of Laughlin and Ellis (1986) and are thus highly intellective. Condition 1 is that the group members must agree on a conceptual system. Elementary arithmetic, algebra, and logic comprise a conceptual system that our college student participants understand and agree upon. Condition 2 is that there must be sufficient information. The previous illustrations demonstrate that informative equations, effective reasoning from the answers to the equations, and effective use of hypotheses will provide sufficient information for problem solution. Condition 3 is that the member(s) who do not know the correct answer should be able to recognize it if it is proposed by another group member. Condition 4 is that the member(s) who do know the correct answer have sufficient ability, motivation, and time to demonstrate it to the incorrect member(s). These four conditions are strongly fulfilled for letters-to-numbers problems. A group member who proposes the substitution of known letters in previous equations to identify unknown letters should be able to demonstrate the algebraic validity of the substitution, and the other members should accept the demonstration. A group member who proposes that multiletter equations with combinations of known letters identify more letters than the simple addition of two known letters should be able to demonstrate this to the other group members, and they should accept the demonstration. A group member who proposes that the equation that adds all ten letters will identify the letters coded as 4 and 5 should be able to demonstrate this to the other group members by the formula for the sum of the integers from 1 to N or by scratch paper arithmetic, and they should accept the demonstration.

In his classic *Group Process and Productivity* Steiner (1972) discussed disjunctive unitary tasks, where each member performs the same task and the group selects the best solution, thereby potentially performing at the level of the best group member. In the current experiment sets of eight participants were randomly assigned to solve the problems as a four-person group or four independent individuals. The best group member should be able to perform as well as the best of the four independent individuals. If the other three group members accept the solution of this best group member on a disjunctive unitary task, the group would be expected to perform at the same level as the best of the four independent individuals. Beyond this, the groups performed better than the best individuals, or, equivalently, better than their best member would perform alone.

In an earlier article Steiner (1966, p. 280) considered complementary tasks: "Complementary models are designed to deal with cases in which the single individual performs only a part of a total task, while other persons, possessing different kinds of resources, perform the remaining parts." Steiner presented models demonstrating that the potential productivity of groups may be greater than the potential productivity of their best member on complementary tasks. Letters-to-numbers problems are such a complementary task on which different group members may possess "different kinds of resources" or insights into informative equations and effective strategies. One member may propose using multiletter equations rather than equations with only two letters. Another group member may have another insight, such as proposing the equation that adds all ten letters. Another group member may propose effective algebraic reasoning, such as subtracting one equation from another. Each group member should be able to demonstrate the effectiveness of his or her insight to the other group members. By combining member contributions of informative equations and effective reasoning according to a complementary model, rather than selecting the single best-member solution according to a unitary disjunctive model, the groups solved the problems in fewer trials than each of the best, second-best, third-best, and fourth-best independent individuals.

GROUPS PERFORM BETTER THAN THE BEST INDIVIDUALS: INFORMATIVE EQUATIONS AND EFFECTIVE STRATEGIES

In an experiment by Laughlin et al. (2003) one hundred three-person groups and three hundred individuals solved two successive letters-to-numbers problems. In addition to the Standard Instructions and procedures of Laughlin, Bonner, and Miner (2002), there were four further instruction conditions that the authors believed would improve performance over the Standard Instructions.

Five Instruction Conditions

Recall from the previous illustrations of strategies the general principle that as the number of letters per equation increases, the equation will identify increasingly more letters. Accordingly, in the Three Letters Instructions the groups or individuals were first given the Standard Instructions and were then told to use at least three letters on each equation (e.g., $A + B + C = ?$, $AA + B = ?$, $A + B + CD = ?$). Similarly, in the Four Letters Instructions the groups or individuals were first given the Standard Instructions and then instructed to use at least four letters on each equation (e.g., $A + B + C + D = ?$, $A + A + A + A = ?$, $AA + B + CD = ?$). The authors predicted that there would be fewer trials to solution for both the Three Letters Instructions and Four Letters Instructions than the Standard Instructions for two reasons. First, the previous discussion and illustrations indicate that as the number of letters per equation increases, the equation will identify increasingly more letters. Second, Laughlin, Bonner, and Miner (2002) found that 49% of the groups, 65% of the best individuals, 72% of the second-best individuals, 77% of the third-best individuals, and 71% of the fourth-best individuals used two-letter equations exclusively over all their trials. Thus the instructions to use at least three or four letters on each equation should counteract the inclination to use a simple two-letter substitution strategy and generate more informative multiletter equations.

In two further Instruction Conditions the authors attempted to improve performance by identifying the coding of one letter to a number at the outset of the problem. In the Number 1 Known Instructions the groups or individuals were first given the standard instructions, and the letter coded as 1 was then identified before beginning the problem. Although this might simply increase the tendency to use a two-letter substitution strategy, the known letter coded as 1 allows the problem to be solved in one trial as demonstrated below, where the letter E is known to be 1 before beginning the problem.

Trial	Equation	Hypothesis	Feedback
1	$E + EE + EEE + EEEE + EEEEE + EEEEEE$	$I = 0$	True
	$+ EEEEEEE + EEEEEEEE + EEEEEEEEE$		
	$= EDAGBFHCJ = 123456789$		

Note: $A = 3, B = 5, C = 8, D = 2, E = 1, F = 6, G = 4, H = 7, I = 0, J = 9$

Similarly, in the Number 9 Known Instructions the groups and individuals were first given the standard instructions and the letter coded as 9 was then identified before beginning the problem. This allows a simple but effective strategy as demonstrated below, where the letter J is known to be 9 at the outset of the problem.

Trial	Equation	Hypothesis	Feedback
1	$J + J = EC$	$A = 0$	False
2	$J + J + J = DH$	$B = 0$	False
3	$J + J + J + J = AF$	$G = 0$	False
4	$J + J + J + J + J = GB$	$I = 0$	True

Note: $A = 3, B = 5, C = 8, D = 2, E = 1, F = 6, G = 4, H = 7, I = 0, J = 9$

These illustrations show that both the known numbers 1 and 9 allow effective strategies that will solve the problem in a maximum of four trials. Accordingly, the authors predicted that there would be fewer trials to solution for the Number 1 Known Instructions and the Number 9 Known Instructions than the Standard Instructions.

The experimental design was a 4 (persons: groups, best individuals, second-best individuals, or third-best individuals) × 5 (instructions: Standard, Three Letters, Four Letters, Number 1 Known, or Number 9 Known) × 2 (problems: 1 or 2) factorial with repeated measures on the third factor, and twenty replications of each of the between-subject conditions. There were twenty random codings of the letters $A, B, \ldots, J$ to the ten numbers $0, 1, \ldots, 9$. In replications 1–10 the first ten of the random codings were used for Problem 1 and the second ten for Problem 2, and in replications 11–20 the second ten codings were used for Problem 1 and the first ten codings were used for Problem 2.

Trials to Solution

The best, second-best, and third-best individuals were determined by the number of trials to solution over the two problems within each set of three individuals for each of the twenty replications for each of the Instruction Conditions.

Figure 6.4 gives the mean trials to solution for Problems 1 and 2 for the groups, best individuals, second-best individuals, and third-best individuals. The groups had significantly fewer trials to solution than each of the best, second-best, and third-best individuals.

Figure 6.5 gives the mean trials to solution for the five Instruction Conditions. There were fewer trials to solution for Number 9 Known Instructions (labeled 9 on the horizontal axis) than each of the other four instructions, fewer trials to solution for Four Letters Instructions (E4) than each of the Standard (Unconstrained or UN) Instructions, Three Letters Instructions (E3), and Number 1 Known Instructions (1), and nonsignificant differences between the Standard, Three Letters, and Number 1 Known Instructions. In summary, there were fewer trials to solution for both the Four Letters and Number 9 Known Instructions than the Standard Instructions, but there were not significantly fewer trials to solution for the Three Letters and Number 1 Known Instructions than the Standard Instructions.

Equations with Minimal Letters

Recall that the groups used equations with more letters than the best individuals in Laughlin, Bonner, and Miner's (2002) previous experiment,

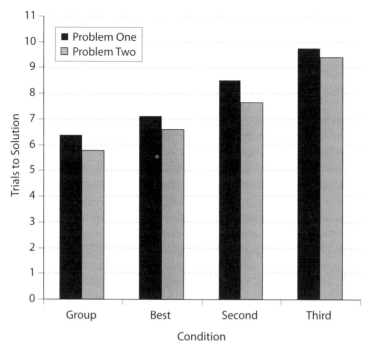

Figure 6.4. Mean Trials to Solution (Laughlin et al. 2003)

and hence identified more letters per equation. The minimal number of letters per equation is two for Standard, Number 1 Known, and Number 9 Known Instructions, three for Three Letters Instructions, and four for Four Letters Instructions, so that equations with more than these minimal letters will be more informative. Figure 6.6 gives the proportions of equations with minimal letters for the groups and best, second-best, and third-best individuals. The groups had a lower proportion of equations with minimal letters than each of the best, second-best, and third-best individuals. Thus the groups used equations with more letters and hence obtained more information than the best individuals.

The mean trials to solution for the five Instruction Conditions were Number 9 Known < Four Letters < (Standard = Three Letters = Number 1 Known). The known number 9 enabled simple but effective strategies such as those of the previous illustration. In contrast, the known number 1 seemed merely to have reinforced the tendency to use a simple but inefficient two-letter substitution strategy starting with the 1. The instructions to use at least four letters per equation generated more informative equations and precluded the use of a simple but inefficient two-letter

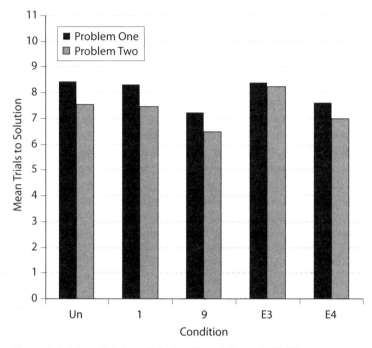

Figure 6.5. Mean Trials to Solution (Laughlin et al. 2003).

substitution strategy. In contrast, there were no significant differences between the Standard Instructions and Three Letter Instructions. Although
the Three Letter Instructions precluded the use of a simple two-letter
substitution strategy, they led to an analogous approach of proposing a
series of equations that added three single letters (e.g., $A + B + C) = ?$;
$D + E + F = ?$, etc.), identifying one or more letters, and then employing
a substitution strategy to identify the remaining letters.

The Number of Persons × Instructions Interaction was not significant,
indicating that the effect of instructions was comparable for groups and
individuals. These results suggest that both collective and individual induction may be improved in two ways. First, the groups or individuals
may be instructed or induced to generate and process more complex
information than their predilections, as by the instructions to use at
least four letters on each equation. These instructions both precluded
the tendency to use simple but inefficient approaches such as a two-
letter substitution strategy and generated more informative equations.
Second, the groups or individuals may be given initial information that
facilitates effective information-processing strategies, as by the known
letter 9.

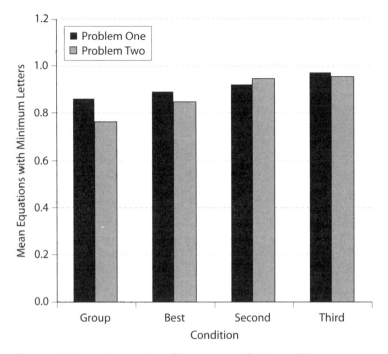

Figure 6.6. Mean Proportion of Equations with Minimal Letters (Laughlin et al. 2003).

GROUPS PERFORM BETTER THAN THE BEST INDIVIDUALS: EFFECTS OF GROUP SIZE

Previous Research on Group Size on Intellective Tasks

In a large early study (Thorndike 1938) students in classes from five universities responded as individuals and then as four-person, five-person, or six-person groups to both factual world knowledge items (e.g., geography, economics. politics) and items with correct answers defined by the judgment of experts (e.g., the better of two poems, the better of two paintings). Four-person groups were correct on 59% of the items, five-person groups on 61%, and six-person groups on 63%, indicating moderate linear improvement with increasing group size. Taylor and Faust (1952) gave individuals, two-person groups, and four-person groups five "Twenty Questions" problems on each of three successive days. Four-person groups solved more of the fifteen problems in the allowed twenty questions than two-person groups, but there was a nonsignificant difference for the number of trials to solution on the solved problems. Lorge and Solomon (1959, 1960) compared various group sizes from two to seven in intact classes in different years on the Tartaglia (husbands and wives) river crossing problem. There was no consistent relationship between percentage of solvers and group size. For example, the solution rate was 15% for three-person groups and 13% for six-person groups in one class, and 66% for four-person groups and 46% for seven-person groups in another class. Similarly, Thomas and Fink (1961) found no significant differences between groups of size two, three, four, and five on the Maier and Solem (1952) horse trading Problem.

Recall from chapter 4 that Laughlin et al. (1975) first gave individual college students the 115 vocabulary items of the Terman (1956) Concept Mastery Test. After dichotomizing the individual scores at the median into high and low halves, they randomly assigned the students within each half to retake the same items as individuals or in cooperative groups of size two, three, four, or five. There was significant linear improvement with increasing group size for the high-ability groups but no effect of group size for the low-ability groups. Bray, Kerr, and Atkin (1978) compared male and female groups of size two, three, six, and ten on "gold dust" problems (modified Luchins's [1942] water jar problems) of low, medium, or high difficulty. For problems of low difficulty there was no difference between group sizes, probably because of a ceiling effect. For problems of moderate difficulty male groups of size ten had more correct answers than groups of sizes three and six, but female groups did not differ significantly from one another. For problems of high difficulty there was no effect of group size, probably owing to a floor effect.

In summary, previous research suggests that performance improves with increasing group size for problems of moderate difficulty requiring understanding of verbal, quantitative, or logical conceptual systems, but performance has not been shown to improve with increasing group size for Eureka problems. Letters-to-numbers problems require knowledge of arithmetic, algebra, and logic and information processing over a series of trials. The previous studies of Laughlin, Bonner, and Miner (2002) and Laughlin et al. (2003) indicate that letters-to-numbers problems are challenging but not excessively difficult for the participants. Thus previous research would suggest improvement with increasing group size.

Recall that Laughlin and colleagues (2002, 2003) proposed that the crucial aspect of the superior group performance over individuals is the use of more complex multiletter strategies rather than the simple, obvious, but less effective two-letter substitution strategies. The 328 individuals in Laughlin, Bonner, and Miner's (2002) study had a probability of .71 of using two-letter equations on all trials for their single problem. The 180 individuals over the Unconstrained, Letter Coded as 1 Given, and Letter Coded as 9 Given Instruction Conditions in Laughlin et al. (2003) had a probability of .67 of using two-letter equations on all trials on their first problem and .65 on their second problem. This gives an overall individual probability of .68 of using two-letter equations on all trials. Assuming that multiletter equations are demonstrably preferable to two-letter equations if proposed by at least one group member, the probability of the groups using a multiletter strategy is $1 - .68^N$ (where N = group size). This predicts probabilities of .54, .69, .79, and .85, respectively, that groups of sizes two, three, four, and five will use a multiletter strategy.

Laughlin et al. (2006) compared groups of size two, three, four, and five and the best of an equivalent number of individuals on letters-to-numbers problems. From the previous review of research on group size and the predicted probabilities that groups of sizes two, three, four, and five will use a multiletter strategy, the authors predicted a major improvement in trials to solution from two-person to three-person groups but progressively decreasing improvement from three-person to four-person to five-person groups.

Experimental Design

The participants were 760 college students. Of these, 200 were randomly assigned to solve two successive letters-to-numbers problems as individuals, 80 as forty two-person groups, 120 as forty three-person groups, 160 as forty four-person groups, and 200 as forty five-person groups. There were twenty random codings of the ten letters to the ten numbers. The Standard Instructions and procedures were the same as those of Laughlin, Bonner, and Miner (2002).

Trials to Solution

The best, second-best, third-best, fourth-best, and fifth-best of the five individuals in each of the forty replications were determined by the number of trials over the two problems (nonsolvers in the allotted ten trials were considered to require eleven trials). Means were 12.98 for the best individuals, 15.00 for second-best, 16.90 for third-best, 18.58 for fourth-best, and 19.78 for fifth-best.

The forty five-person groups were compared to the forty best, second-best, third-best, fourth-best, and fifth-best individuals. Four of the five individuals in each replication were randomly selected and the forty four-person groups were compared to the forty best, second-best, third-best, and fourth-best of these four individuals. Similarly, three of the five individuals in each replication were randomly selected and the forty three-person groups were compared to the forty best, second-best, and third-best of these three individuals, and two of the five individuals in each replication were randomly selected and the forty two-person groups

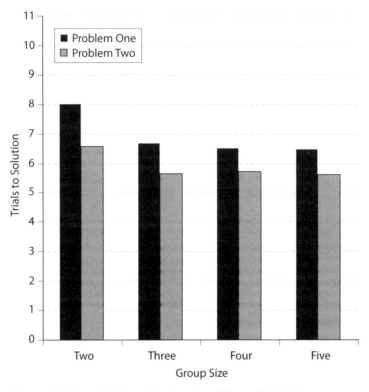

Figure 6.7. Mean Trials to Solution (Laughlin et al. 2006)

were compared to the forty best and second-best of these two individuals.
Figure 6.7 gives the mean trials to solution for two-person, three-person,
four-person, and five-person groups.

The main effect of group size was significant, and pairwise comparisons
indicated fewer trials to solution for each of three-person, four-person,
and five-person groups than two-person groups, with nonsignificant differences between three-person, four-person, and five-person groups. Figures 6.8 and 6.9 give the trials to solution for two-person groups and
the best and second-best individuals; three-person groups and the best,
second-best, and third-best individuals; four-person groups and the best,
second-best, third-best, and fourth-best individuals; and five-person
groups and the best, second-best, third-best, fourth-best, and fifth-best
individuals. Each of the three-person, four-person, and five-person
groups had significantly fewer trials to solution than the corresponding
best individuals. The two-person groups performed at the level of the
best of two individuals and better than the second-best individuals.

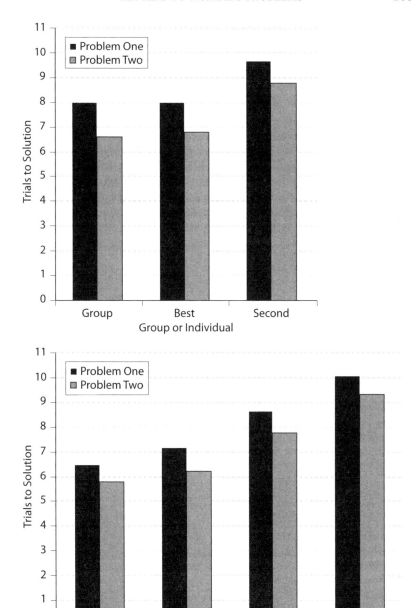

Figure 6.8. Mean Trials to Solution for Groups and Two Individuals (top) and Groups and Three Individuals (bottom) (Laughlin et al. 2006).

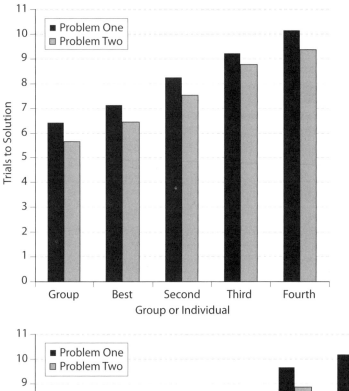

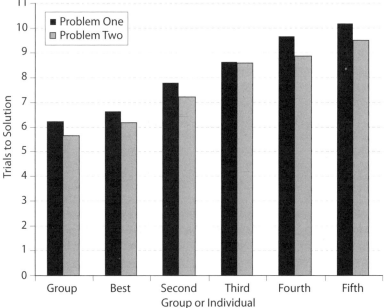

Figure 6.9. Mean Trials to Solution for Groups and Four Individuals (top) and Groups and Five Individuals (bottom) (Laughlin et al. 2006)

These results suggest that groups of size three are necessary and sufficient to perform better than the best of an equivalent number of individuals on intellective problems. Previous research had suggested that performance improves with increasing group size for problems of moderate difficulty requiring understanding of verbal, quantitative, or logical conceptual systems but not on insight or Eureka problems. The finding that three-person groups performed better than two-person groups is consistent with this research, since letters-to-numbers problems require understanding of arithmetic, algebra, and logic and systematic reasoning over a series of trials rather than a single insight, and they are of moderate but not excessive difficulty for intelligent and motivated college students.

Why was there no further improvement as group size increased from three to four to five? The authors suggested that the crucial aspect of effective performance on letters-to-numbers problems is the use of multiletter equations to identify two or more letters per equation rather than using a simple but inefficient two-letter substitution strategy that identifies only one letter per trial. The individual probability of using two-letter equations in previous research and the assumption that multiletter equations are demonstrably preferable to two-letter equations if proposed by at least one group member predicts progressively smaller improvement with increasing group size. Coordination difficulties (Steiner 1972) and production blocking (Diehl and Stroebe 1987, 1991; Valacich, Dennis, and Connolly 1994) may also have increased with increasing group size beyond three members. Although these processes should be minimal in three-person groups, they may be more detrimental in four-person and five-person groups. However, observation of the groups did not suggest evidence of motivation loss from three-person groups to four-person and five-person groups because of free-riding (Kerr 1983; Olson 1965).

Why Do Groups Perform Better Than the Best Individuals on Letters-to-Numbers Problems?

In three experiments, three-person, four-person, and five-person groups performed better than the best of an equivalent number of individuals. We attribute this superiority to the highly intellective nature of letters-to-numbers problems, which allow recognition and adoption of correct responses, recognition and rejection of erroneous responses, and effective collective information processing (Hinsz, Tindale, and Vollrath 1997; Laughlin, VanderStoep, and Hollingshead 1991). Letters-to-numbers problems strongly fulfill the four conditions of demonstrability of Laughlin and Ellis (1986). First, the group members understand and agree on the underlying conceptual systems of arithmetic, algebra, and logic.

Second, there is sufficient information to demonstrate the superiority of strategies such as multiletter equations relative to obvious but less effective two-letter substitution strategies, and to demonstrate and reject erroneous inferences. Virtually any sequence of equations of any degree of complexity contains some information, and the groups were able to process this information more effectively than the best individuals. Third, the member(s) who had not considered effective strategies and reasoning recognized their effectiveness when they were proposed by other member(s). Fourth, the member(s) who proposed the effective strategies and reasoning had the ability, motivation, and time to demonstrate the effectiveness to the other member(s). Thus the group members combined their abilities and resources to perform better than the best of an equivalent number of individuals on the highly intellective complementary group task.

Tindale and Kameda (2000) and Kameda, Tindale, and Davis (2003) generalized the first of these four conditions of demonstrability in their concept of *social sharedness*, the degree to which preferences and cognitions are shared among group members at the outset of group interaction. Building upon these shared preferences (the objective of solving in as few trials as possible and the norms of interpersonal influence such as accepting a demonstrably effective strategy) and cognitions (the conceptual systems and operations of arithmetic, algebra, and logic), the groups combined the abilities, skills, and insights of their members and thus performed better than the best of an equivalent number of individuals.

Letters-to-numbers problems combine aspects of hypothesis testing (e.g., Klayman and Ha 1987), mathematical and logical reasoning (e.g., Laughlin and Ellis 1986; Stasson et al. 1991), cryptographic reasoning from given information rather than by generating further evidence (e.g., Newell and Simon 1972; Singh 1999), and collective induction (e.g., Crott, Giesel, and Hoffman 1998; Laughlin 1996, 1999). These different aspects combine in an interesting problem that is challenging and motivating for intelligent college students.

The groups were able to overcome the common knowledge effect (e.g., Gigone and Hastie 1993, 1997) and hidden profile effect (e.g., Stasser and Titus 1985, 1987, 2003) where groups discuss common initial preferences and shared information, fail to discuss unique unshared information, and hence make suboptimal decisions. In contrast to this research, where a single member with critical information may not be able to convince other members of the validity of the information, the highly intellective nature of letters-to-numbers problems enables members who propose informative equations and an effective strategy to demonstrate the effectiveness of the strategy to the other group members. Evidence is presented in chapter 7 that effective group performance on letters-to-numbers problems also results in member learning that transfers to subsequent effective individual problem solving.

Chapter Seven

GROUP-TO-INDIVIDUAL
PROBLEM-SOLVING TRANSFER

MANY SCIENTIFIC, educational, business, military, and political groups assume that people who solve problems in groups and teams will solve subsequent problems better as individuals than people without previous group problem-solving experience. This is the fundamental issue of group-to-individual transfer. The transfer problem may be the same as the training problem, defining *specific* group-to-individual transfer, or a new problem of the same general class, defining *general* group-to-individual transfer.

Both specific and general group-to-individual transfer may be assessed in a three-stage IGI versus III design. In the IGI experimental condition participants solve problems as individuals (I), then as groups (G), and then as individuals (I). In the III control condition the participants solve the same problems three times as individuals. Group-to-individual transfer is demonstrated by better third-stage performance for individuals in the IGI condition than in the III condition. This IGI versus III design also allows assessment of group versus individual problem solving on the second administration, and also model-fitting analyses of the social combination processes by which the groups map known distributions of correct and incorrect members on the first administration to a correct or incorrect group response (Kerr, Stasser, and Davis 1979).

SPECIFIC TRANSFER

Analogies

Laughlin and Adamopoulos (1980) assessed specific group-to-individual transfer with an IGI versus III design for three administrations of the same thirty verbal analogy problems of the form $A : B :: C : D$, with five possible multiple-choice answers for D. Example items were:

Sink: Float :: Iron: Heavy, Wood, Fight, Metal, Water
Speedometer: Rapid :: Thermometer: Mercury, Temperature, Coldness, Hot, Weather
Cotton: Silk :: Plant: Fiber, Cocoon, Thread, Worm, Spin

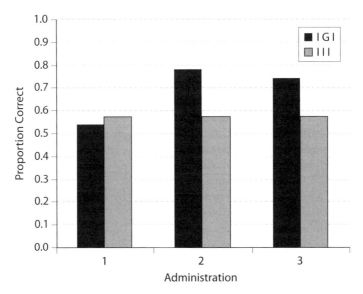

Figure 7.1. Proportion of Correct Analogies (Laughlin and Adamopoulos 1980)

College students first took the thirty items alone (I), with no time limit. Their answer sheets were then collected, and they were randomly assigned to either six-person groups (G) or control individuals (I) for the second administration of the same thirty items with new answer sheets. The groups were instructed to discuss each item and decide on a common group answer. No decision scheme such as unanimity or majority was imposed or implied by the instructions. Following this the answer sheets were collected, and all participants took the same thirty items again as individuals (I).

Figure 7.1 gives the proportion of correct answers for the IGI and III conditions for the three administrations. As indicated in Figure 7.1, the individuals in the IGI and III conditions did not differ significantly on the first administration, as would be expected from the random assignment to the IGI and III conditions. The groups had a significantly higher proportion of correct answers than the individuals on the second administration. Because there was an equal number of groups and individuals, this would be expected from the well-demonstrated superiority of groups over the average individual on intellective tasks (recall the references in chapter 2). The individuals in the IGI condition performed better than the individuals in the III condition on the third administration, indicating positive group-to-individual transfer. Because these problems were the

TABLE 7.1
Observed Social Decision Scheme for Group on
Second Administration over All Analogy Items

Member		Group	
Correct	Incorrect	Correct	Incorrect
6	0	1.00	.00
5	1	.99	.01
4	2	.96	.04
3	3	.90	.10
2	4	.67	.33
1	5	.28	.72
0	6	.05	.95

Source: Laughlin and Adamopoulos 1980.

same as the second administration, this is *specific* group-to-individual transfer.

Table 7.1 gives the obtained social decision scheme for the groups on the second administration. As indicated in Table 7.1, the groups were highly likely to propose correct answers if at least three group members were correct as individuals, and there was a probability of .67 if two members were correct. However, the probability of a correct answer when only one member was correct was only .28, close to the expected probability of a correct answer by guessing with five response alternatives. The predictions of unanimity, 5/6 majority, 4/6 majority, proportionality, equiprobability, truth-supported-wins, and truth-wins models were tested against the obtained group responses. The truth-supported-wins model could not be rejected, and all other models were rejected. Thus two correct members were necessary and sufficient for a correct group response.

Mathematical Problems

Laughlin and Ellis (1986) used an IGI versus III design for three administrations of the same ten elementary algebra, geometry, and probability problems. Individuals first took the ten problems alone and were then randomly assigned to five-person groups or control individual conditions for the second administration of the same problems. Finally, all participants took the same ten items again as individuals.

Figure 7.2 gives the proportion of correct answers for the IGI and III conditions for the three administrations. As indicated in Figure 7.2, the

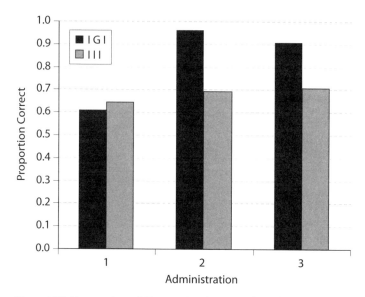

Figure 7.2. Proportion of Correct Mathematical Problems (Laughlin and Ellis 1986)

individuals in the IGI and III conditions did not differ significantly on the first administration, as would be expected from the random assignment to the IGI and III conditions. The groups had a significantly higher proportion of correct answers than the individuals on the second administration, again as would be expected from the demonstrated superiority of groups over the average individual in problem solving. The individuals in the IGI condition performed better than the individuals in the III condition on the third administration, indicating positive group-to-individual transfer. Because these problems were the same as the second administration, this is *specific* group-to-individual transfer.

Table 7.2 gives the obtained social decision scheme for the groups on the second administration. As indicated in Table 7.2, the groups were highly likely to propose correct answers if at least two group members were correct as individuals, and there was a high probability of .83 when only one member was correct. The predictions of unanimity, 4/5 majority, 3/5 majority, proportionality, equiprobability, truth-supported wins, and truth-wins models were tested against the obtained group responses. The truth-wins model could not be rejected, and all other models were rejected. Thus one correct member was necessary and sufficient for a correct group response. This contrasts with the necessary two correct members on vocabulary, analogy, and general information world knowledge

TABLE 7.2
Observed Social Decision Scheme for Group on
Second Administration over All Mathematical Items

Member		Group	
Correct	Incorrect	Correct	Incorrect
5	0	1.00	.00
4	1	.99	.01
3	2	.97	.03
2	3	.97	.03
1	4	.83	.17
0	5	.50	.50

Source: Laughlin and Ellis 1986.

problems, and indicates the relatively greater demonstrability of mathematical problems than world knowledge problems.

General Transfer

Mathematical Problems

Stasson et al. (1991) used an IGI versus III design with five algebra, geometry, and probability problems for the first two administrations, and then new problems that could be solved by the same general principle or equation on the third administration. Individuals first took the five problems alone, and then, for the second administration of the same problems, they were randomly assigned to five-person groups or control individual conditions. Then all participants took five new problems as individuals on the third administration.

Figure 7.3 gives the proportion of correct answers for the IGI and III conditions for the three administrations. As indicated in Figure 7.3, the individuals in the IGI and III conditions did not differ significantly on the first administration, as would be expected from the random assignment to the IGI and III conditions. The groups had a significantly higher proportion of correct answers than the individuals on the second administration, again as would be expected from the demonstrated superiority of groups over the average individual in problem solving. The individuals in the IGI condition performed better than the individuals in the III condition on the third administration, indicating positive group-to-individual transfer. Because these problems were different from the second administration, this demonstrates *general* group-to-individual transfer.

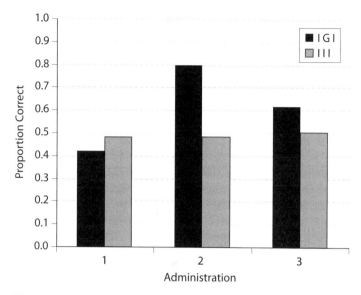

Figure 7.3. Proportion of Correct Mathematical Problems (Stasson et al. 1991)

Table 7.3 gives the obtained social decision scheme for the groups on the second administration. As indicated in Table 7.3, the groups were highly likely to propose correct answers if at least two group members were correct as individuals, and there was a probability of .65 when only one member was correct. The predictions of unanimity, 4/5 majority, 3/5 majority, proportionality, equiprobability, truth-supported wins, and truth-wins models were tested against the obtained group responses. The predictions of the truth-wins model could not be rejected, indicating that one correct member was necessary and sufficient for a correct group response. Again, this contrasts with the necessary two correct members on vocabulary, analogy, and general information world knowledge problems, and indicates the relatively greater demonstrability of mathematical problems than world knowledge problems.

Brainteasers

Olivera and Straus (2004) used an IGI versus III design with the same brainteasers such as hidden word problems for the first two administrations, and then new brainteaser problems that could be solved by the same general approach on the third administration. The groups solved the problems better on the second administration, and the individuals in

TABLE 7.3
Observed Social Decision Scheme for Group on
Second Administration over All Mathematical Items

Member		Group	
Correct	Incorrect	Correct	Incorrect
5	0	1.00	.00
4	1	1.00	.00
3	2	.98	.02
2	3	.88	.12
1	4	.65	.35
0	5	.31	.69

Source: Stasson et al. 1991.

the IGI condition solved the problems better on the third administration than the III individuals, again demonstrating general group-to-individual transfer. Olivera and Straus did not report social combination analyses, but we would expect a good fit for a truth-wins model because of the highly demonstrable nature of the brainteasers.

Logical Implication

Recall from chapter 5 that, in Study 1, Maciejovsky and Budescu (2007) used a three-stage IGI design in which individuals solved new logical implication problems in Stage 3 after solving as a cooperative group in Stage 2. Some of the participants received the same problem in Stage 3 that they had in Stage 1 (assessing specific transfer) and some received eight new problems (assessing general transfer). Only the participants who had failed to solve their problem in Stage 1 were considered. Thirty percent of these participants who received one problem in Stage 3 solved the problem, indicating specific group-to-individual transfer. Participants who received eight problems in Stage 3 solved 25% of the problems, indicating general group-to-individual transfer.

In Study 2 the participants received eight new problems in Stage 3 after participating in a competitive auction with feedback on bids and earnings in Stage 2. Participants who had received public feedback in the auction solved 49% of the problems, indicating general group to-individual transfer.

In Study 3 the participants received eight new problems in Stage 3 after participating in Stage 2 with two, one, or no insiders (those who had solved the implication problem as individuals in Stage 1) in a competitive auction without feedback on bids and earnings. Twenty-three percent of the problems were solved with two insiders, 15% with one insider, and 7% with no insiders.

In summary, many participants who had failed to solve an implication problem alone in Stage 1 solved new problems alone after participating in a cooperative group or in different types of competitive auctions, demonstrating general group-to-individual transfer.

FOUR ISSUES IN GROUP-TO-INDIVIDUAL TRANSFER

All these studies used a single training session and a single transfer session. Consequently all five studies assessed two issues: (a) group versus individual training performance; and (b) group-to-individual transfer. If there is more than one training session, two further issues arise: (c) sufficiency; and (d) completeness. *Sufficiency* is the issue as to whether one training session is sufficient for group-to-individual transfer. *Completeness* is the issue as to whether group-to-individual transfer is complete, that is, whether individual performance on the transfer problems is at the level of performance by comparably experienced groups on the same problems.

An experiment by Laughlin, Carey, and Kerr (2008) assessed these four issues of group-to-individual problem-solving transfer on letters-to-numbers problems. The problems were presented on a computer terminal, and there were some modifications of the procedure with a human experimenter in Laughlin et al.'s three previous letters-to-numbers studies (2002, 2003, 2006) that we have considered in chapter 6. After the group or individual proposed an expression (equation) in letters (e.g., $C + G$) the program computed and displayed the value of the expression (answer) (e.g., $C + G = ED$). The group or individual then entered a coding for the number $0, 1, \ldots, 9$ corresponding to a letter for as many of the ten letters as desired (in contrast to the previous three experiments where only one hypothesis was proposed per trial). The computer then indicated whether the hypotheses were correct or incorrect. Hence there were four stages on each trial: (a) formulating and entering an expression; (b) reasoning from the computer-generated value of that expression; (c) assigning a number to one or more of the remaining unidentified letters; and (d) reasoning from the provided feedback that the assignment of numbers to letters was correct or incorrect. Figure 7.4 is an illustration of the computer screen during a problem.

The researchers expanded the traditional GI versus II design to include three GGGI, GGII, and GIII conditions in which the participants solved three, two, or one problems as a group before solving one, two, or three

Trial	Expression	Value	Guess									
			A	B	C	D	E	F	G	H	I	J
1	C+G	ED			7	3	1		8			
2	E+E	D				2	1	3	0	4	5	6
3	D+DDD+EDE	AGB	3	5		2	1	9	4	6	8	7
4	EDA+BBB	FHC	3	5	8	2	1	6	4	7	7	0
5	E+C	J	3	5	8	2	1	6	4	7	0	9
6												
7												
8												
9												
10												

Correct

Wrong

Figure 7.4. Computer Screen during Problem Solution (Laughlin, Carey, and Kerr 2008).

problems as individuals. The researchers also expanded the traditional II condition to an IIII control condition in which the participants solved four successive problems as individuals. Further expanding the traditional IG vs. II design, the researchers included a GGGG group control condition in which the participants solved four successive problems as a group.

Contrasts of the group and individual conditions within each of the four problems address the four issues of group-to-individual transfer. First, do groups perform better than individuals? Second, does positive group-to-individual transfer occur? Third, is a single group experience sufficient for a full group-to-individual transfer effect, or is extended group experience essential? Fourth, is group-to-individual transfer complete, that is, at the level of group performance, or does limited prior group experience produce only limited individual improvement? Figure 7.5 summarizes sixteen contrasts that address these four issues. The bottom part of Figure 7.5 includes a check mark under the particular contrasts and weights that test Hypotheses 1, 2, 3, and 4.

| | Problem | | | | | | | | | | | | | | | |
| | 1 | 2 | | | 3 | | | | | 4 | | | | | | |
Contrast	1	2	3	4	5	6	7	8	9	10	11	12	13	14	15	16
GGGG	−1	−1	−1	0	0	0	−1	−1	0	0	0	−1	0	0	0	−3
GGGI	−1	−1	−1	0	0	0	−1	−1	0	0	0	0	0	−1	−1	1
GGII	−1	−1	−1	0	0	−1	1	0	−1	−1	0	0	−1	0	0	1
GIII	−1	3	0	−1	−1	1	1	0	0	0	−1	0	1	1	0	1
IIII	4	0	3	1	1	0	0	2	1	1	1	1	0	0	1	0

Contrast relevant to hypothesis? (√ means yes)

	1	2	3	4	5	6	7	8	9	10	11	12	13	14	15	16
G > I	√		√					√				√				
Transfer				√	√				√	√	√					√
Sufficient							√						√	√		
Complete		√					√									√

Figure 7.5. Contrasts to Test Four Hypotheses (Laughlin, Carey, and Kerr 2008)

Hypothesis 1: Groups will perform better than individuals. Better performance for groups than individuals is a likely (if not necessary) prerequisite for positive group-to-individual transfer. As indicated in Contrast 1 of Figure 7.5, Hypothesis 1 is tested on Problem 1 by comparison of (GGGG, GGGI, GGII, and GIII) versus IIII, with respective weights of −1 for each of GGGG, GGGI, GGII, and GIII, and 4 for IIII. Similarly, Hypothesis 1 is tested on Problem 2 by comparing the three conditions that solve the first two problems as a group (GGGG, GGGI, and GGII) and the IIII condition that solves the first two problems as an individual (Contrast 3), with respective weights of −1 for each of GGGG, GGGI, and GGII, 0 for GIII, and 3 for IIII. Hypothesis 1 is tested on Problem 3 by comparing (GGGG and GGGI) and IIII (Contrast 8); and on Problem 4 by comparing GGGG and IIII (Contrast 12).

Hypothesis 2: Positive group-to-individual transfer will occur. As illustrated in chapter 6, letters-to-numbers problems entail demonstrably effective approaches, strategies, and generalizations that may be learned during group problem solving, either by one group member from another or as emergent insights that none of the group members would have realized alone (see Laughlin, Bonner, and Miner 2002; and Laughlin et al. 2003). These approaches, strategies, and generalizations should be transferable to subsequent individual problem solving. Hence the authors expected positive group-to-individual transfer, in which individuals with previous group experience perform better than individuals without previous group experience. As indicated in Figure 7.5, Hypothesis 2 is tested on Problem 2 by comparing GIII and IIII (Contrast 4); on Problem 3 by comparing GIII and IIII (Contrast 5) and GGII and IIII (Contrast 9); and on Problem 4 by comparing GGII and IIII (Contrast 10), GIII and IIII (Contrast 11), and GGGI and IIII (Contrast 15).

Hypothesis 3: One previous group experience is sufficient for positive group-to-individual transfer to occur. Because previous groups have been demonstrated to use effective approaches, strategies, and generalizations on letters-to-numbers problems (Laughlin, Bonner, and Miner 2002; Laughlin et al. 2003; 2006), the authors hypothesized that solving one problem as a group would be sufficient for the members to learn such effective approaches, strategies, and generalizations that would transfer to subsequent individual problem solving. Thus the GIII individuals who have solved one previous problem as a group should perform as well on Problem 3 as the GGII individuals who have solved two previous problems as a group (Contrast 6). Similarly the GIII individuals who have solved one previous problem as a group should perform as well on Problem 4 as the GGII individuals who have solved two previous problems as a group (Contrast 13), and the GIII individuals who have solved one previous problem as a group should perform as well on Problem 4 as the GGGI individuals who have solved three previous problems as a group (Contrast 14). Significant differences for these contrasts would indicate that more than one group experience is necessary for positive group-to-individual transfer and help identify just how much prior experience is required.

Hypothesis 4: Group-to-individual transfer will be complete. Hypotheses 2 and 3 assess the occurrence and sufficiency of group-to-individual transfer by comparing individuals who have had previous group problem solving experience to individuals who have not had previous group problem solving experience. Hypothesis 4 is the stronger prediction that strategies and generalizations learned while solving a single problem as a group should be fully understood by the group members and consequently result in subsequent individual problem solving at the level of group problem solving on the same problem. As indicated in Figure 7.5, Hypothesis 4 is tested on Problem 2 by comparing (GGGG, GGGI, GGII) and GIII (Contrast 2); on Problem 3 by comparing (GGGG, GGGI) and (GGII, GIII) (Contrast 7); and on Problem 4 by comparing GGGG and (GGGI, GGII, GIII) (Contrast 16).

Design

The participants were 525 college students. There were five experimental conditions defined by group (G) problem solving or individual (I) problem solving for four successive problems: GGGG, GGGI, GGII, GIII, and IIII. The participants in the GGGG condition solved four successive problems as a three-person group; the participants in the GGGI condition solved three problems as a group at one terminal, and each person then solved one problem as an individual at a separate terminal; the participants in the GGII condition solved two problems as a group and two problems as individuals; and the participants in the GIII condition solved one problem as a group and three problems as individuals.

In Condition GIII the three persons who had previously been in a group on Problem 1 solved Problems 2, 3, and 4 as individuals. Similarly, in Condition GGII the three persons who had previously been in a group on Problems 1 and 2 solved Problems 3 and 4 as individuals, and in Condition GGGI the three persons who had previously been in a group on Problems 1, 2, and 3 solved Problem 4 as individuals. Thus the number of trials to solution for these individuals may not have been independent. In order to test for nonindependence the authors computed the intraclass correlations on each of Problems 2, 3, and 4, as recommended by Kenny, Kashy, and Bolger (1998) and Kenny et al. (2002). These intraclass correlations were .38, .33, and .31 for Problems 2, 3, and 4, respectively. According to these authors, an intraclass correlation of .10 indicates nonindependence, and "if there is nonindependence, then group not person must be used as the unit of analysis" (Kenny, Kashy, and Bolger 1998, p. 239). Accordingly, the authors computed the means for the three persons who had previously been in a given group (Problems 2, 3, and 4 for GIII, Problems 3 and 4 for GGII, and Problem 4 for GGGI), giving thirty-five scores for the respective problems in these conditions. Because the individuals in the IIII condition were completely independent of one another, the authors did not average over these sets of three individuals.

Table 7.4 gives the means and the results of the sixteen contrasts directly testing Hypotheses 1, 2, 3, and 4. All contrasts were tested with the error term for the respective problem.

Hypothesis 1. Groups will perform better than individuals. As indicated in Table 7.4, Contrast 1 testing group versus individual performance on Problem 1, Contrast 3 on Problem 2, Contrast 8 on Problem 3, and Contrast 12 on Problem 4 were all significant, supporting Hypothesis 1 and indicating that the groups performed better than the control individuals on each of Problems 1, 2, 3, and 4. This superiority of group over individual problem solving is a highly likely, if not necessary, prerequisite for positive group-to-individual transfer to occur, although some members could conceivably learn something during group problem solving even if the groups did not perform better than the individuals.

Hypothesis 2. Positive group-to-individual transfer will occur. As indicated in Table 7.4, Contrast 4 testing for group-to-individual transfer

TABLE 7.4

Tests of Four Hypotheses for Trials to Solution (G = Group, I = Individual)

Hypothesis	Problem	Contrast and Means on Trials to Solution	$F\,(1, 240)$	$p <$
G > I	One	(#1) (GGGG, GGGI, GGII, GIII) 5.90 vs. IIII 7.91	42.70	.001
	Two	(#3) (GGGG, GGGI, GGII) 4.66 vs. IIII 6.67	43.70	.001
	Three	(#8) (GGGG, GGGI) 4.60 vs. IIII 6.14	21.89	.001
	Four	(#12) GGGG 3.91 vs. IIII 5.75	26.81	.001
Transfer	Two	(#4) GIII 5.48 vs. IIII 6.67	7.67	.01
	Three	(#5) GIII 4.95 vs. IIII 6.14	8.13	.01
		(#9) GGII 5.08 vs. IIII 6.14	6.54	.01
	Four	(#10) GGII 4.91 vs. IIII 5.75	5.69	.05
		(#11) GIII 4.99 vs. IIII 5.75	4.61	.05
		(#15) GGGI 5.03 vs. IIII 5.75	4.15	.05
Sufficient	Three	(#6) GGII 5.08 vs. GIII 4.95	< 1	
	Four	(#13) GGII 4.91 vs. GIII 4.99	< 1	
		(#14) GGGI 5.03 vs. GIII 5.75	< 1	
Complete	Two	(#2) (GGGG, GGGI, GGII) 4.66 vs. GIII 5.48	3.63	
	Three	(#7) (GGGG, GGGI) 4.60 vs. (GGII, GIII) 5.01	1.32	
	Four	(#16) GGGG (3.91) vs. (GGGI, GGII, GIII) 4.97	8.93	.01

Note: Contrast numbers are based on Figure 7.5.
Source: Laughlin, Carey, and Kerr 2008.

on Problem 2, Contrasts 5 and 9 on Problem 3, and Contrasts 10, 11, and 15 on Problem 4 were all significant. This supports Hypothesis 2 and demonstrated consistent positive group-to-individual transfer: individuals with varying previous group experience consistently performed better than control individuals without any previous group experience.

Hypothesis 3. One previous group experience is sufficient for positive group-to-individual transfer to occur. As indicated in Table 7.4, Contrast 6 testing for sufficiency on Problem 3 and Contrasts 13 and 14 testing for sufficiency on Problem 4 were not significant: the GIII individuals who had previously solved one problem in a group performed as well on Problem 3 as the GGII individuals who had previously solved two problems in a group. Similarly, the GIII individuals who had solved only one problem as a group performed as well on Problem 4 as the GGII individuals who had previously solved two problems as a group and the GGGI individuals who had previously solved three problems as a group. These results confirm Hypothesis 3 and indicate that one previous group experience was sufficient for positive group-to-individual transfer to occur for the letters-to-numbers problems.

Hypothesis 4. Group-to-individual transfer will be complete. As indicated in Table 7.4, the GIII individuals did not differ significantly from the GGGG, GGGI, and GGII groups on Problem 2 (Contrast 2). Similarly, the GGII and GIII individuals did not differ significantly from the GGGG and GGGI groups on Problem 3 (Contrast 7). This indicates that group-to-individual transfer on Problems 2 and 3 was complete, or at the level of group performance. However, the GGGI, GGII, and GIII individuals did not perform as well as the GGGG groups on Problem 4 (Contrast 16). This indicates that although positive group-to-individual transfer occurred on Problem 4, it was not up to the level of the GGGG controls who solved all four problems as a group. Thus Hypothesis 4 was supported for Problems 2 and 3 but not for Problem 4.

In summary, (a) groups performed better than individuals; (b) positive group-to-individual transfer occurred; (c) one group experience was sufficient for positive group-to-individual transfer to occur; and (d) group-to-individual transfer was complete, or at the level of group performance, on Problems 2 and 3 but not on Problem 4.

These results provide strong evidence on the four issues of positive group-to-individual problem-solving transfer. First, the groups performed better than the individuals, which is a basic requisite for positive group-to-individual transfer. Second, individuals with previous group experience consistently performed better than individuals without previous group experience, demonstrating positive group-to-individual transfer. Third, one group experience was sufficient for the group-to-individual transfer effect to occur, demonstrating sufficiency. In other words, for this task, all the benefit that came from prior group experience was obtained through one's first such experience. Finally, transfer was at the level of group performance on Problems 2 and 3, demonstrating the completeness of transfer, but was less than group performance on Problem 4, on which the group performance was exceptional.

SUMMARY

The studies of Laughlin and Adamopoulos (1980) and Laughlin and Ellis (1986) demonstrated *specific* group-to-individual transfer to the same problems, and the studies of Stasson et al. (1991), Olivera and Straus (2004), and Maciejovsky and Budescu (2007) demonstrated *general* group-to-individual transfer to new problems of the same class that could be solved by the same procedures. The superior performance of groups over individuals in all five studies provided a basis for the incorrect group members to learn from the correct members, and this learning transferred to their individual problem solving. In these studies there was only one training session and one transfer session, addressing the issues of group versus individual performance and group-to-individual transfer. The subsequent study of Laughlin, Carey, and Kerr (2008) used one, two, or three training sessions, addressing the two further issues of sufficiency and completeness of transfer. One training session was sufficient for transfer, and transfer was complete to Problems 2 and 3 but not to Problem 4, for which the performance of the groups was exceptional.

Many educational, business, medical, military, and other systems assume both specific and general group-to-individual transfer. Together with the studies in the previous chapters, these results indicate that this assumption is warranted: groups are not only more effective problem-solving systems than individuals, but this problem-solving experience in groups fosters member learning that transfers to subsequent individual problem solving.

Chapter Eight

SOCIAL CHOICE THEORY

IN THE PREVIOUS CHAPTERS we have considered social combination models of the processes by which group members combine their different preferences in a collective group response. Social choice theory in economics and political science considers how the members of a society such as voters or policy makers may make societal decisions such as selection among competing candidates to office or policies by existing or possible voting systems. Thus social combination models and social choice theory address the same basic issue: the aggregation of group member preferences to a collective group response.

Contemporary social choice theory was inspired by two seminal books: *The Theory of Committees and Elections* by the Scottish political economist Duncan Black (1958) and *Social Choice and Individual Values* by the American welfare economist Kenneth Arrow (1963 [1951]). Black's presentation of social choice theory is descriptive, and analytic, considering the nature and consequences of existing parliamentary procedure and voting systems. Black first presented his own theory in part 1 of *The Theory of Committees and Elections*. He then considered the "History of the Mathematical Theory of Committees and Elections" in part 2. As a result of historical scholarship in the London Museum, Oxford and Cambridge Universities, and Paris, he rediscovered and elaborated the forgotten work on voting of the French theorists the Marquis de Condorcet and Jean-Charles de Borda in the eighteenth century, and the British mathematician Charles Dodgson (Lewis Carroll) in the nineteenth century.

Arrow's presentation of social choice theory is normative, axiomatic, and deductive, and is expressed in both symbolic logic form and fuller explanations. Arrow came from a background in welfare economics, and he distinguished *tastes,* or matters of consumption, and *values,* which adds individual standards of equity. As indicated by his title, he was basically concerned with values. In accordance with our distinction between intellective tasks and judgmental tasks, values are thus matters of judgmental preference rather than demonstrable truth. Beginning with two axioms and four definitions, he then proposes five desirable characteristics of a social welfare function and considers whether existing or possible voting systems achieve them. This led to his famous impossibility theorem.

In this chapter we present some basic ideas of social choice theory and voting systems using Black's descriptive formulation and present evidence for social choice theory from experimental research on group decision making.

Basic Concepts of Social Choice Theory

Black (1958) defines committees and elections as correlative terms: a *committee* is a group of people, face-to-face as a parliamentary body or distributed as an electorate, who make a collective decision among alternatives by a procedure of voting. A *motion* is a proposal before a committee. He presents a framework for representing individual and collective preference orders for both continuous alternatives such as allocation of money and discrete alternatives such as choice among candidates.

Motions (Alternatives) and Preference Orders

Black represents individual preference orders for members A, B, C . . . for alternatives $a_1, a_2, a_3, \ldots$, as a vertical line, with the most preferred alternative highest on the line. An individual preference order may then be plotted on the vertical axis against the ordered alternatives on the horizontal axis. However, it is more convenient to follow Riker (1982) in representing motions (alternatives) as $x, y, z, \ldots$, rather than subscripted $a_{i,}$ and a preference order as a row rather than a column, with the most preferred alternative on the left. For example, three voters might have the preference orders A $x\,y\,z$, B $x\,z\,y$; C $y\,z\,x$.

For-Against Matrices

Like Dodgson (1874), Black used a for-against matrix to organize the results of pairwise choice for three or more members and alternatives. Each alternative is a row and column of the matrix, and the cell entries are the ordered pair of votes that the row and column alternatives receive when the row alternative is voted against the column alternative. Thus the for-against matrix for the three previous preference orders is the following:

		Against		
		x	*y*	*z*
	x	—	2,1	2,1
For	*y*	1,2	—	2,1
	z	1,2	1,2	—

Because the entries below the major diagonal are a reflection of the entries above the major diagonal, it is sufficient to enter only the first member of each ordered pair.

			Against	
		x	y	z
	x	—	2	2
For	y	1	—	2
	z	1	1	—

Sequential Pairwise Voting and the Paradox of Voting

The Marquis de Condorcet (1795/1995) was a French mathematician, a political theorist, and a statesman. During his tenure as Secretary of the Royal Paris Academy of Science, Condorcet controlled both the procedures for admission to the Academy and the publications of the Academy. In this capacity he proposed a method of election to membership by making all pairwise choices between alternatives. Condorcet proposed that the alternative that obtains a majority against each other alternative by pairwise vote should be the social choice. The alternative (if any) that defeats all the other alternatives by pairwise voting is called the *Condorcet winner*.

Consider the three preference orders A: $x\ y\ z$; B: $z\ x\ y$; C: $y\ z\ x$: The for-against matrix is the following:

			Against	
		x	y	z
	x	—	2	1
For	y	1	—	2
	z	2	1	—

The *agenda* specifies the order of pairwise votes. With the agenda $x\ y\ z$ the decision is z:

Step 1	Winner	Step 2	Winner
x vs. y	x	x vs. z	z

With the agenda x z y the decision is y:

Step 1	Winner	Step 2	Winner
x vs. z	z	z vs. y	y

With the agenda $y\,z\,x$ the decision is x:

Step 1	Winner	Step 2	Winner
y vs. z	y	y vs. x	x

Thus the decision is z, y, or x depending upon the agenda. The for-against matrix indicates that each alternative defeats one alternative and is defeated by one alternative: x defeats y, y defeats z, and z defeats x, so there is no Condorcet winner. A collective preference order of this type is called a *cycle* or *cyclical majority*. The most elementary cycle results from one of the twelve possible 3 × 3 Latin Squares in which no alternative appears more than once in the same row or the same column. With more than three alternatives there may be full cycles involving all alternatives, partial cycles involving fewer than all alternatives, or cycles within cycles. When there is a cycle, the later an alternative enters the voting, the more likely that it will be the collective choice or group decision.

Sequential pairwise voting is the procedure followed by many decision-making groups such as parliaments, senates, or faculty meetings. An alternative is presented as a main motion, which may be amended and replace the main motion, and a defeated motion is not considered further. Black called this the Ordinary Committee Procedure, or Procedure Alpha. He considers two other possibilities, Procedure Beta and Procedure Gamma, varying the point at which alternatives are voted against each other by a Condorcet procedure and the point where the final motion is voted against the status quo of no change. He presents several theorems on the possibility of agenda manipulation. An individual or subgroup that controls the meeting agenda may be able to achieve a favored decision by arranging the agenda so that an alternative that could defeat the favored alternative will be defeated by some other alternative in an earlier pairwise vote.

A fascinating example of avoiding the paradox of voting by procedural rules occurred at the Constitutional Convention. On the opening day of the Convention, May 25, 1787, a Committee consisting of George Wythe of Virginia, Alexander Hamilton of New York, and Charles Pinckney of South Carolina was appointed to prepare standing rules and orders. The Committee reported on May 28, and fourteen rules were adopted. Richard Spaight of North Carolina then moved "that the House might not be precluded by a vote on any question from revisiting the subject matter of it, when they see cause, nor, on the other hand, be led too hastily to rescind a decision which was the result of mature discussion." The motion was referred to the Committee, which reported on May 29, and the following rule was adopted.

> That a motion to reconsider for a matter which has been determined by a majority, may be made, with leave, unanimously given, on the same day on

which the vote passed; but otherwise, not without one day's previous notice, in which last case, if the House agree to reconsideration, some future day shall be assigned for that purpose. (Farrand 1911, Vol. 1, p. 17)

Runoff Elections

A runoff election has two stages. In the first stage each voter has one vote for any of three or more candidates. If a candidate has a majority of these votes, the candidate is elected. If no candidate has a majority, all candidates except the two receiving the highest number of votes are eliminated. A second runoff election is then conducted between the two candidates who received the most votes.

It is possible for a Condorcet winner to lose with a runoff election. Consider the following preference orders for five voters and three candidates, x, y, z:

$$A, B \quad x\,z\,y$$
$$C, D \quad y\,z\,x$$
$$E \quad z\,x\,y:$$

		Against		
		x	y	z
	x	—	3	2
For	y	2	—	2
	z	3	3	—

In the first stage the number of first-place votes is as follows:

$$x: \quad 2$$
$$y: \quad 2$$
$$z: \quad 1$$

Candidate z with only one vote is eliminated. In the runoff stage, candidate x receives three votes and candidate y receives two votes, so candidate x is the winner. However, candidate z is a Condorcet winner who could defeat each of x and y in pairwise votes.

Rank Order Voting

Black also rediscovered and discussed the work on voting of Jean-Charles de Borda, another member of the Royal Paris Academy of Science who was also an artillery officer before the French Revolution and a sea captain as well (McLean and Urken 1995). Borda (1781) proposed a rival method of election to the Academy, which was adopted in 1784 and used until 1800 (Black 1958, p. 180). Each voter rank orders each candidate from most to least favored. For each voter the highest-ranked candidate (alternative) receives $n - 1$ points, the second-highest $n - 2$ points, the third-highest $n -3$ points, and so forth, to the lowest-ranked alternative, which receives 0 points. The points for each alternative are then summed across voters, and the alternative with the highest sum is the decision. To illustrate, assume the following rankings for five voters and four alternatives:

A	w	x	y	z
B	y	z	x	w
C	x	y	z	w
D	w	x	y	z
E	y	w	x	z

The computations are:

	A	B	C	D	E	Total
w	3	0	0	3	2	8
x	2	1	3	2	1	9
y	1	3	2	1	3	10
z	0	2	1	0	0	3

Alternative y, with a total of 10 points, is the decision. The procedure is called the Borda count, and the actual point total for each alternative is called the Borda score.

Another way to compute the Borda count when the highest-ranked alternative is given $n - 1$ points is to sum over each row of the for-against matrix:

			Against			
		w	x	y	z	Sum
	w	—	3	2	3	8
For	x	2	—	3	4	9
	y	3	2	—	5	10
.	z	2	1	0	—	3

There may be a different Condorcet winner and Borda winner, as follows:

A	x	y	v	w	z
B	y	v	z	w	x
C	z	x	y	v	w
D	x	y	w	z	v
E	y	w	v	x	z

		Against					
		v	w	x	y	z	Sum
	v	—	3	2	0	3	8
	w	2	—	2	0	3	7
For	x	3	3	—	3	3	12
	y	5	5	2	—	4	16
	z	2	2	2	1	—	7

Alternative x is the Condorcet winner. Alternative y is the Borda winner.

Approval Voting

In contrast to majority/plurality voting systems that consider only voter-first preferences, the Borda count considers the ranking of all alternatives. Approval voting is a more recent system that may also incorporate more than first preferences. In approval voting, each voter may give one vote to as many alternatives as desired. The alternative with the most votes is selected. To illustrate, again assume the previous preference orders:

A	x	y	v	w	z
B	y	v	z	w	x
C	z	x	y	v	w
D	x	y	w	z	v
E	y	w	v	x	z

Assume that voter A approves of x and y; B approves of y only; C approves of z, x, and y; D approves of x, y, and w; and E approves of y, w, v, and x. This gives the following approval votes:

v	w	x	y	z
1	2	4	5	1

Alternative y, with the most approval votes, is the collective choice. Approval voting is widely used to select members to professional or honorary associations and to sports halls of fame. Different types of approval-voting systems may be used to select more than one alternative (say, three) or to limit the number of approval votes (say, to two alternatives). Brams and Fishburn (1983) give an extensive treatment of approval voting and indicate many advantages, such as giving voters more flexibility in expressing their preferences and a greater likelihood of electing a more generally favored candidate than single-vote majority/plurality winner-take-all systems.

The Median Voter Theorem

In a famous theorem Black (1958) proved that if the committee member preference orders can be ordered on one dimension on the horizontal axis (say, allocation of money) and are single-peaked (rising to a point and then falling), then the median motion (alternative) can defeat all other alternatives by pairwise votes. Moreover, Black demonstrated that sequential pairwise voting between adjacent alternatives, 1 vs. 2, 2 vs. 3, 3 vs. 4, and so on, rather than all pairwise votes will have the same effect.

Black further considered majority voting if the collective preference order is not single-peaked, decisions under special (higher-order) majorities, and changing orders of majorities (for example, passage of legislation by a simple majority but overrule of a veto by a two-thirds majority). Political scientists have analyzed the records and procedures of decision-making bodies such as the U.S. Senate and House of Representatives for evidence of Black's concepts of cycles, single-peaked collective preference orders, agenda and parliamentary manipulation, and special majorities (see Grofman 1981, for a comprehensive review).

Condorcet Jury Theorem

Although best remembered for pairwise voting between alternatives, Condorcet also attempted to develop a probabilistic theory of group decision making (McLean and Urken 1995). In this endeavor he proposed what Black (1958) later called the *Condorcet jury theorem*. As summarized by McLean and Urken (1995, p. 6) the Condorcet jury theorem entails three assumptions:

1. Voters are expressing their considered judgments on whether a claim is true or false (rather than simply voting for what is in their interests).
2. Each voter forms his or her judgment independently of the others.
3. Each voter is on the average right more often than wrong, even if only by a small margin.

Grofman and Owen (1986, p. 94) formalize the Condorcet jury theorem as follows:

$$P_N = \sum_{b=m}^{N} \binom{N}{b} p^b (1 - p)^{N-b}$$

Where P_N is the majority judgment of a group of size N, m is the size (order) of majority, and p is the member probability of being correct with $p > .5$). The equation sums the appropriate terms of the binomial expansion of $(p + (1 - p))^N$ and so the probability of a correct majority judgment increases with both group size and member probability of being correct. Several chapters in Grofman and Owen (1986) consider extensions of the Condorcet jury theorem.

EXPERIMENTAL EVIDENCE FOR SOCIAL CHOICE THEORY

The Median Voter Theorem

Preference among Bets. Crott, Zuber, and Schermer (1986) tested Black's median voter theorem for all pairwise comparisons, Black's reduced pairwise comparisons for adjacent ordered alternatives (1 vs. 2, 2 vs. 3, 3 vs. 4, etc.) model, and fifteen social combination models (e.g., Davis 1973; Laughlin 1980), such as proportionality and equiprobability, for group decisions among bets. The bets varied both the probability of winning and the amount of money (in Deutsch marks) with the same expected value. There were three sets of bets—Set I, Set II, and Set III—with six bets with equally spaced probability values and six bets with equally spaced money values. For example, in Set I the six bets with equally spaced probability values were .25 * 18.00, .35 * 12.80, .45 * 9.90, .55 * 8.20, .65 * 6.90, and .75 * 6.00, and the six bets with equally spaced money values were .24 * 18.50, .28 * 16.00, .33 * 13.50, .41 * 11.00, .53 * 8.50, and .75 * 6.00. Individuals first rank ordered the six bets in one of Sets I, II, or III. The researchers then composed groups of five persons with three types of distributions of first preferences: (a) 2 1 1 1 0 0 with variations (e.g., 2 0 1 0 1 1) and mirror images; (b) 2 2 1 0 0 0 with variations (e.g., 0 2 0 2 1 0) and mirror images; and (c) 2 1 2 0 0 0 with variations (e.g., 0 2 1 0 2 0) and mirror images. The groups then discussed the six bets and made a collective decision. The procedure of individual and group decisions was then repeated for the other two of Sets I, II, and III.

The best-fitting model by Wilcoxon matched pairs tests for predicted versus obtained group decisions was the Black reduced paired comparison model for single-peaked distributions and the median if the distribution was not single peaked.

Choice Dilemmas. Zuber, Crott, and Werner (1992) tested Black's reduced paired comparisons median model and nine social combination models for two Choice Dilemma Questionnaire items in which participants first individually chose one of nine levels of acceptable odds of success for a more desirable outcome, 1/10, 2/10, etc. (see, e.g., Burnstein 1982 and Myers and Lamm 1976 for reviews of the large group choice shift and group polarization literature with these items). In addition to this typical choice of one alternative, the participants rank ordered the alternatives, allowing assessment of the Borda model.

The researchers then composed five-person groups without a majority for one alternative, such as a 21011 group in which two members favored alternative 1/10 and one member each favored alternatives 2/10, 4/10, and 5/10. The groups then made a collective decision. The researchers tested the Black reduced paired comparison median model, the Borda model, and seven models from a previous experiment by Laughlin and Earley (1982) which had dichotomized the 10-point scale into 1–5 risky and 6–10 conservative: proportionality, plurality, equiprobability, risk wins, risk supported wins, conservative wins, and conservative supported wins. The models were tested by Wilcoxon signed ranks tests, corrected for ties. The Black reduced paired comparison median model provided the best fit for each of three experimental conditions designed to assess persuasive arguments theory (e.g., Burnstein 1982) and over all three conditions. Nine other models, including Borda rank order, were rejected.

Political Scenarios. Crott, Szilvas, and Zuber (1991) tested the Black median model and ten other models for group decisions on a choice dilemma item (whether to go to medical school or become a professional musician), a political item (number of refugees to be granted asylum), and a role-playing item to determine the distance for the location of a proposed school. On the choice dilemma item there were five probabilities of success: .1, .3, .5, .7, and .9. On the asylum item there were seven possible numbers of refugees to be allowed entry: 5,000, 9,000, 13,000, 17,000, 21,000, 25,000, and 29,000. On the school location item there were seven possible distances in kilometers: 5, 10, 15, 20, 25, 30, and 35. Individuals first responded to the items and then were composed in five-person groups under the constraints that there was not a majority preference and the distribution was skewed.

The Black median model again provided the best fit, and Borda, proportionality, mean, plurality, equiprobability, risk wins, risk-supported wins, conservative wins, and conservative-supported wins were rejected.

Damage Awards for Mock Civil Juries. Davis et al. (1997) had participants first view a videotape of a mock personal injury civil trial and decide on the appropriate amount of a damage award from 0 to 1 million dollars. They then discussed the case in six-person or twelve-person juries and made a collective decision. A trimmed median model, in which the most extreme low or high individual preference was ignored, provided the best fit for the group decision.

Hypothetical Foragers. Hastie and Kameda (2005) integrated social choice and social combination models with evolutionary psychology theory in computer simulations of the decision processes of hypothetical foragers. They used a test bed with ten locations varying in value (amount/quality) and groups of five or twelve foragers. Individual foragers integrated cues to form estimates of the values of the locations, and these estimates were then combined by nine group aggregation algorithms. The first four of these required the group to operate on the individual forager estimates for the values of the ten locations. These rules were (a) averaging; (b) median; (c) Davis (1996) social judgment model, which assumes that the influence of one member on another decreases with the difference between their preferences as a negative exponential function; and (d) the Borda method. The second five of these rules did not require this stage of group operations on the individual forager values but considered only their first-choice preferences. These were (e) unique Condorcet winner; (f) one of tied Condorcet pairwise winners; (g) majority, plurality otherwise; (h) best member; and (i) random member. Individual forager opportunity loss was computed by subtracting the value of the forager's first-choice location from the value of the best location.

There was less opportunity loss for the four decision rules that required a group operation on the values of all locations than the five decision rules that considered only first-choice preferences. The best of the four rules was averaging. The majority/plurality rule performed the best of the five rules that considered only the first-choice preferences. The Condorcet winner and the Borda rule performed well, which supports Black's analyses for decision methods that consider all alternatives rather than just the first choice

Agenda Influence

Purchase of Airplanes by a Flying Club. Levine and Plott (1977) and Plott and Levine (1978) reported a remarkable demonstration of the power of setting the agenda for a group decision. The authors were members of a flying club that owned a fleet of small airplanes that were rented hourly to the club members. The club was planning to replace their fleet with six or seven new airplanes and the decision had been narrowed to four different types, identified by the authors as A, C, E, and F, which varied on cost, speed, passenger capacity, and configurations. The members differed considerably in their preferences, and the authors had definite preferences:

Our most preferred alternative was a seven-plane fleet consisting of three E's, plus either two more E's or two F's, and two C's. We were particularly anxious to have at least one C included (it has six seats, while E's and F's have only four), and we wished to avoid including A's (they have six seats, but are too expensive for us). Our ordering then was (where ~ indicates indifference):

(1) EEEEECC ~ EEEFFCC
(2) EEEEEC ~ EEEFFC
(3) EEEEEA ~ EEEFFA
(4) EEEEEAA ~ EEEFFAA (Levine and Plott 1977, pp. 572–573)

A formal meeting of the club members was called to make recommendations to the Board of Directors, and one of the authors was appointed to set the agenda so that the decision could be made in an orderly manner. From a previous questionnaire and meetings he had considerable knowledge of the individual member preferences, and most seemed to favor a fleet consisting entirely of E's or F's, without C's. Believing that both the content and order of decisions were important, he constructed the following agenda of sequential decisions:

(1) What type of airplane should the primary fleet be? This was to be decided by a Borda count (rank order point voting).
(2) How many planes do we want?
(3) Do we want a mixed fleet?
(4) What type of aircraft should our secondary fleet be?
(5) How elaborately should we equip the aircraft we purchase? (p. 579)

In addition to manipulating the agenda, the authors also manipulated the voting rule by the initial Borda count to determine the type of airplane for the primary fleet: "The Borda count was used rather than simple balloting because we did not want the group to become aware of the pattern of controversy and thus vote more strategically" (Levine and Plott 1977, p. 576). The second decision was whether to have an unmixed or mixed fleet, decided by a show of hands (mixed won). Subsequent decisions were structured as pairwise choices by the ordinary parliamentary procedure. The third decision was six versus seven airplanes (seven won). The fourth decision was no secondary fleet versus a secondary fleet (secondary won). The fifth decision was between EEEEECC and EEEEEAA. There was a tie and the Board of Directors chose EEEEECC because the C's were less expensive than the A's.

In summary, the authors achieved their preferred decision by setting the agenda and selecting the voting rules. They discuss possible applications of agenda setting to the House of Representatives, the Supreme Court, appellate and administrative courts, and jury deliberations. Riker

(1982, 1986) gives several historical examples of agenda setting. A particularly interesting case is the structure of successive decisions by which Gouverneur Morris achieved a change at the Constitutional Convention in 1787 from an originally approved proposal for Congress to elect the president to the Electoral College system eventually adopted.

Joined Charges in a Mock Jury Trial. Several charges against a defendant may be joined in a single jury trial. In a mock jury study by Davis et al. (1984) there were three charges against the defendant: criminal damage to property (least serious), aggravated battery (intermediate seriousness), and reckless homicide (most serious). After watching a videotaped presentation of trial evidence as individuals and giving their judgment of acquittal or conviction, six-person juries considered the three charges in an order of ascending seriousness (criminal damage to property, aggravated battery, reckless homicide) or descending seriousness (reckless homicide, aggravated battery, criminal damage to property). The proportion of convictions for the intermediate aggravated battery charge was higher for the descending order, in which the most serious charge had previously been considered, than the ascending order, in which the least serious charge had previously been considered, indicating the effect of the agenda order on the group decisions.

Policy Allocations. In an agenda study by Nadler et al. (2001) four-person groups in the role of a policy committee made three recommendations for the allocation of funds for AIDS treatment to (a) a city, (b) a region of the state that included the city, or (c) the state. Allocations were made in two agenda orders: (a) city, region, state; or (b) state, region, city. Allocations in the increasing order (city, region, state) were larger than allocations in the decreasing order (state, region, city), indicating the effect of the two agenda orders.

In summary, Condorcet's method of voting by pairwise comparisons led to his discovery of the "paradox of voting," in which the order of pairwise decisions determine the outcome of decisions for nontransitive collective preference orders. Black both rediscovered Condorcet's forgotten work on the paradox of voting and considered other possibilities of agenda influence with sequential pairwise decisions. Experimental research on agenda effects supports Black's analysis by demonstrating that the composition and order of successive group decisions may determine the outcome of the decision.

Condorcet Jury Theorem

Following determinations by the U.S. Supreme Court in *Johnson v. Louisiana* (1972) and *Apodaca v. Oregon* (1972) that the Sixth Amendment did not require unanimous jury verdicts for conviction in noncapital criminal cases, a number of social psychological experiments assessed the effects of distributions of predeliberation jury member preferences (12 guilty, 0 not guilty; 11 guilty, 1 not guilty, etc.) on the jury verdict. In a meta-analysis of twelve such studies MacCoun and Kerr (1988) found verdicts of conviction in 67% of the juries with an initial majority of members who favored conviction, and verdicts of acquittal in 94% of the juries with an initial majority of members who favored acquittal. They concluded that there was both a majority effect and an asymmetrical leniency bias that favored acquittal when there was no majority.

Subsequently Devine et al. (2001) aggregated the data of these twelve studies and fourteen other studies. For those juries that reached a verdict (excluding hung juries) majorities of 9, 3 or greater convicted in 100% of the cases, majorities of 8, 4 convicted in 63% of the cases, and majorities of 7, 5 convicted in only 29% of the juries. Majorities of 4, 8 or greater for acquittal prevailed in all but one jury. Similarly majorities of 5, 1 convicted in 97% of the juries but majorities of 4, 2 in only 70%, whereas majorities of 2, 4 acquitted in 96% of the juries and majorities of 1, 5 in 99%.

In summary, meta-analyses of jury decision making support Black's analysis by demonstrating both strong overall majority effects and an increasing majority effect with increasing orders of majorities. There is a break between strong 9, 3 majorities and weaker 8, 4 majorities for conviction in twelve-person juries and a break between strong 5, 1 majorities and weak 4, 2 majorities for conviction in six-person juries. Simple (weak) majorities for acquittal prevail in both twelve-person and six-person juries. These results are consistent with Black's theoretical analyses of "special" majorities. (Black, 1948a 1948b).

Successive Majorities in a Hierarchical System

A logical extension of the Condorcet jury theorem is the effect of successive majorities in a hierarchical structure, where successive majority decisions, with the majority winner going on to the next level, will exaggerate the original preference distribution. As a simple illustration, assume a population of twenty-seven voters who are members of the Blue and Green parties. The twenty-seven voters are randomly distributed in nine three-member Precincts; the nine Precincts are organized in three Districts; and the three Districts are organized in one Region. Nine elections are held at the Precinct level, and the nine winners go on to their respective Districts, where another election is held. The three District winners go on to the Region level for the final election. At each level there is a two-thirds majority decision rule. Hence there are four possible types of member distributions in Precincts and Districts:

Blue	Green
3	0
2	1
1	2
0	3

Assume a population of nineteen Blues and eight Greens, with respective probabilities of .7037 and .2963. The binomial expansion of $(.7037 + .2963)^3$ gives the probabilities of occurrence of the four types of Precincts as .3485, .4402, .1853, and .0260. Applying the two-thirds majority decision rule by summing .3485 and .4402 gives a predicted probability of .7887 Blue winners at the Precinct level, and summing .1853 and .0260 gives a predicted probability of .2113 Green winners at the Precinct level. Substituting these new probabilities in the binomial expansion and applying the two-thirds majority decision rule gives predicted probabilities of .8849 Blue winners and .1150 Green winners at the District level. Again substituting these probabilities in the binomial expansion and applying the two-thirds majority decision rule gives a predicted probability of .9631 of a Blue decision and .0366 of a Green decision at the Region level.

Thus initial majorities are progressively exaggerated in such a hierarchical system. Moreover, the greater the number of levels, the greater the exaggeration. Likewise, the greater the initial difference in preferences, the greater the exaggeration. This is a logical consequence of applying the binomial expansion to the probabilities of the two initial preferences, applying the majority decision rule, substituting the resulting probabilities in the next application of the binomial expansion and again applying the majority decision rule, and so on.

This simple illustration assumed random assignment of voters to the initial Precinct level. If the minority Green party controls the assignment of individuals to the Precinct level, it may control the final decision by gerrymandering. Gerrymandering is a process of "cracking" by placing a minimal majority of party members in some initial units (here Precincts) and "packing" by placing as many opposition party members as possible in other units. Hence gerrymandering is a process of "winning small" and "losing big." Moreover, with control of assignment to initial units, progressively smaller proportions of a minority party can control the final decision as the number of hierarchical levels increases. The necessary proportion is the decision rule to the power of the number of levels, for example, $(2/3)^4$ with a four-level system and a two-thirds decision rule at each level.

Ono et al. (1988) conducted "thought experiments" (computer simulations) of the effects of six decision rules in a hierarchical system. Although their simulation was motivated as a deductive test of Likert's

(1961, 1967) inductively posed system 4 or linking pin theory of organizations rather than a logical extension of the Condorcet jury theorem, it is formally equivalent. In Likert's theory there are hierarchical organization levels, say, executive vice president (top), department, division, section, and unit (bottom). Linking pin members belong to two levels, such that they are both the head of a group of subordinates and also a member of a group of peers who meet with their own supervisors, where they presumably pass on the opinions and preferences of their subordinates. According to the theory, this facilitates the communication of opinions and preferences through successive levels, so that a veridical distribution of opinions and preferences is eventually represented at the top.

Ono et al. used the notation and matrix operations of Davis's (1973) social decision scheme theory to test the effects at successive levels of six different social decision schemes (choice rules): (a) equiprobability, which assumes that each response alternative advocated by at least one member is equiprobable as the group decision; (b) proportionality, which assumes that the group chooses an alternative with a probability equal to the proportion of members who advocate it; (c), plurality, equiprobability otherwise; (d) plurality, proportionality otherwise; (e) majority, equiprobability otherwise; and (f) majority, proportionality otherwise. In addition to the binomial case for two alternatives, they simulated the multinomial cases for three and six alternatives, as well as different probabilities of initial preferences for alternatives.

The strict equiprobability decision scheme reduced the initial variability of preferences. The proportionality decision scheme recovered the initial preference distribution. Each of the plurality, equiprobability otherwise; plurality, proportionality otherwise; majority, equiprobability otherwise; and majority, proportionality otherwise decision schemes exaggerated the initial preference distribution. Contrary to the linking pin theory, if "democratic" majority or plurality decision schemes with equiprobability or proportionality subschemes are applied at the successive levels, the initial preference distributions will not be represented at the top level.

A REMARKABLE CONCURRENCE

The president of the American Psychological Association is elected annually by the members of the Association. Each member rank orders five candidates, and the ballots are analyzed by the Hare system. Regenwetter et al. (2007) obtained the ballots for four separate elections and reanalyzed them by Condorcet, Borda, and simple plurality procedures. Remarkably, all three procedures selected the actual winner chosen by the Hare system for all four elections. Moreover, there was no evidence of cyclical majorities. These data sets were very large and constituted the preference orders of a wide variety of psychologists (cognitive, social, clinical, etc.), and insincere (strategic) voting seems unlikely.

SOCIAL CHOICE THEORY AND GROUP PROBLEM SOLVING: THE CONSTITUTIONAL CONVENTION OF 1787

Social choice theory addresses the basic issue of how members of a society solve the problem of making collective decisions by existing or possible voting systems. As a historical example, the representatives from the American colonies who met at the Constitutional Convention of 1787 faced a multitude of judgmental issues on the composition, powers, and procedures of their government. Over four months they achieved consensus on the U.S. Constitution. This consensus integrated a wide range of proposals based on English law, British and continental philosophy, the existing Articles of Confederation, colony charters and constitutions, and the framers' many original ideas. The first three articles of the Constitution specify legislative, executive, and judicial branches, and the methods of direct or indirect social choice systems to select their members.

Recall that the first condition of demonstrability is agreement on a conceptual system. Once this consensus on judgmental issues was achieved, the U.S. Constitution became a conceptual system and guide for group problem solving for subsequent generations of Americans. Constitutions move judgmental issues toward the intellective end of the group task continuum.

Chapter Nine

CONCLUSIONS

IN CONCLUSION we propose ten generalizations that are supported by the theory and research in the previous eight chapters on group problem solving. We end with a brief retrospective and prospective.

GENERALIZATIONS

Group tasks are ordered on a continuum anchored by intellective and judgmental tasks. *Intellective tasks* have a demonstrably correct solution within a mathematical, logical, scientific, or verbal conceptual system. *Judgmental tasks* are evaluative, behavioral, or aesthetic judgments for which no generally accepted demonstrably correct answer exists. Intellective tasks are matters of truth and the objective for the group is to achieve the correct answer; judgmental tasks are matters of value and the objective for the group is to achieve consensus.

The underlying basis of the intellective-judgmental continuum is a continuum of *demonstrability*. Demonstrability requires (a) agreement on a conceptual system, (b) sufficient information, (c) sufficient knowledge of the system by incorrect members to recognize correct solutions, and (d) sufficient ability, motivation, and time for the correct group members to present the solution to the incorrect members.

The proportion of group members that is necessary and sufficient for a group response is inversely proportional to the demonstrability of the proposed response.

Groups perform moderately better than the average individual on recognition and recall memory tasks, and group memory in jury decisions is better than juror memory. Group memory may be improved by transactive memory systems, which are based on the motivational principle of *cognitive interdependence,* where each person's outcomes depend on a combination of his or her own performance and the performance of the other person and the learning principle of *convergent expectations* of which persons know or will learn what.

When information favoring a suboptimal decision is distributed to all group members to learn prior to a group decision (shared information) and unique information favoring an optimal decision is distributed to different members (unshared information or hidden profile), groups tend to discuss the shared information rather than integrate the unique information and hence make the suboptimal decision. This tendency may be reduced by posing the situation as a problem to be solved rather than a judgment, and by appointing each member as an expert on the respective unique information, providing social validation for information known only to one person.

Group performance on world knowledge tasks is proportional to the number of high-ability group members. Overall high-ability groups consist of more heterogeneous members than overall medium-ability or low-ability groups.

In collective induction, groups perform at the level of the best of an equivalent number of individuals. There is a complex but orderly social combination process; multiple evidence is relatively more important than multiple hypotheses; and positive hypothesis tests are relatively more effective than negative hypothesis tests.

Groups perform better than the best of an equivalent number of individuals on highly intellective letters-to-numbers problems and use more complex and insightful strategies.

There is both specific and general transfer from group problem solving to subsequent individual problem solving.

Social combination models in social psychology and social choice theory address the same fundamental issue of aggregation of member preferences to a collective response by voting and procedural systems. Experimental research in social psychology supports some of the propositions of social choice theory.

RETROSPECTIVE AND PROSPECTIVE

From 1930 to 1970 issues of small group performance, including group learning, group problem solving, group decision making, group structure and process, coalition formation, bargaining, negotiation, and intergroup relations were considered under the superordinate term *group problem solving*.

After 1970, following the discovery of the choice shift, Supreme Court decisions allowing juries of fewer than twelve persons and less than unanimity in noncapital criminal cases, emphases on heuristics and biases, and formulations of prospect theory (Kahneman, Slovic, and Tversky 1982; Kahneman and Tversky 1979), the predominant interest of research and theory was decisions under risk and uncertainty. Issues of small group performance were considered under the superordinate term *group decision making*.

Currently increasing globalization of economic and communication systems has led to increasing interest in multidisciplinary and multicultural problem solving *teams* in organizational behavior, business administration, management, and experimental economics. There has been productive discipline-to-discipline transfer from the theories and methods of experimental social psychology on *group problem solving* to multidisciplinary and multicultural *team problem solving.*

The terminology of problem solving or decision making, groups or teams, and social combination or social choice varies, but the fundamental issue remains the same: How is a distribution of member beliefs or preferences aggregated in a collective response?

REFERENCES

Allen, V. L. (1965). Situational factors in conformity. In L. Berkowitz (Ed.), *Advances in experimental social psychology*, Vol. 2 (pp. 133–175). New York: Academic Press

Amar, A. R. (2005). *America's Constitution*. New York: Random House.

Apodaca v. Oregon, 406 U. S. 404 (1972).

Archer, E. J. (1960). A re-evaluation of the meaningfulness of all possible CVC trigrams. *Psychological Monographs, 74* (Whole No. 479).

Arrow, K. J. (1963 [1951]). *Social choice and individual values*. 2nd Ed. New York: Wiley.

Asch, S. E. (1956). Studies of independence and conformity: A minority of one against a unanimous majority. *Psychological Monographs* 70, no. 9 (Whole No. 417).

Ballew v. Georgia, 435 U. S. 223 (1978).

Baron, R. S., and Kerr, N. L. (2003). *Group process, group decision, group action*. 2nd Ed. Philadelphia, PA: Open University Press.

Black, D. (1948a). On the rationale of group decision making. *Journal of Political Economy, 56,* 23–34.

———. (1948b). The decisions of a committee using a special majority. *Econometrica, 16,* 245–261.

———. (1958). *The theory of committees and elections*. Cambridge: Cambridge University Press.

Borda, J-C. (1781). *Memoires sur les élections au scrutin*. Paris: Histoire de l'Academie Royale des Sciences. Translated and edited by I. McLean and A. B. Urken, *Classics of social choice*. Ann Arbor, MI: University of Michigan Press, 1995.

Brams, S. J., and P. C. Fishburn. (1983). *Approval voting*. Boston: Birkhauser.

Bray, R. M., N. L. Kerr, and R. S. Atkin. (1978). Effects of group size, problem difficulty, and sex on group performance and member reactions. *Journal of Personality and Social Psychology, 36,* 1224–1240.

Brown, R. (2002). *Group processes*. 2nd Ed. Oxford, UK: Blackwell.

Burnstein, E. (1982). Persuasion as argument processing. In H. Brandstatter, J. H. Davis, and G. Stocker-Kreichgauer (Eds.), *Group decision making* (pp. 103–124). London: Academic Press.

Clark, N. K., and G. M. Stevenson. (1989). Group remembering. In P. B. Paulus (Ed.), *Psychology of group influence* (2nd Ed., pp. 357–392). Hillsdale, NJ: Erlbaum.

Condorcet, M. (1785). *Essai sur l'application d'analyse a la probabilite des decisions rendes a la pluralite des voix*. Paris: Histoire de l'Academie Royale des Sciences. Translated and edited by I. McLean and A. B. Urken, *Classics of social choice*, Ann Arbor: University of Michigan Press, 1995.

Crott, H. W., M. Giesel, and C. Hoffman. (1998). The process of inductive inference in groups: The use of positive and negative hypothesis and target testing in sequential rule-discovery tasks. *Journal of Personality and Social Psychology*, 75, 938–952.

Crott, H. W., K. Szilvas, and J. A. Zuber. (1991). Group decision, choice shift, and polarization in consulting, political, and local political scenarios: An experimental investigation and theoretical analysis. *Organizational Behavior and Human Decision Processes*, 49, 22–41.

Crott, H. W., J. A. Zuber, and T. Schermer. (1986). Social decision schemes and choice shift: An analysis of group decisions among bets. *Journal of Experimental Social Psychology*, 22, 1–21.

Davis, J. H. (1969). *Group performance*. Reading, MA: Addison-Wesley.

———. (1973). Group decision and social interaction; A theory of social decision schemes. *Psychological Review, 80*, 97–125.

———. (1992). Some compelling intuitions about group consensus decisions, theoretical and empirical research, and interpersonal aggregation phenomena: Selected examples, 1950–1990. *Organizational Behavior and Human Decision Processes, 52*, 3–38.

———. (1996). Group decision making and quantitative judgments: A consensus model. In E. Witte and J. H. Davis (Eds.), *Group decision making: Consensual action by small groups*, 1:35–59.

Davis, J. H., L. Hulbert, W-T. Au, X-P. Chen, and P. Zarnoth. (1997). Effects of group size and procedural influence on consensual judgments of quantity: The example of damage awards and mock civil juries. *Journal of Personality and Social Psychology, 73*, 703–718.

Davis, J. H., P. R. Laughlin, and S. S. Komorita. (1976). The social psychology of small groups: Cooperative and mixed-motive interaction. *Annual Review of Psychology, 27*, 501–541.

Davis, J. H., R. S. Tindale, D. H. Nagao, V. B. Hinsz, and B. Robertson. (1984). Order effects in multiple decisions by groups: A demonstration with mock juries and trial procedures. *Journal of Personality and Social Psychology, 47*, 1003–1012.

Deutsch, M., and H. E. Gerard. (1955). A study of normative and informational social influences upon individual judgments. *Journal of Abnormal and Social Psychology, 51*, 629–636.

Devine, D. J., E. D. Clayton, B. B. Dunford, R. Seying, and J. Fryer. (2001). Jury decision making: 45 years of empirical research on deliberating groups. *Psychology, Public Policy, and Law, 7*, 622–727.

Diehl, M., and W. Stroebe. (1987). Productivity loss in brainstorming groups: Toward the solution of a riddle. *Journal of Personality and Social Psychology, 53*, 497–509.

———. (1991). Production loss in idea-generating groups: Tracking down the blocking effect. *Journal of Personality and Social Psychology, 61*, 392–403.

Dodgson, C. L. (1874). *Suggestions on the best methods of taking votes, when more than two issues are to be voted on*. Oxford, UK: Hall and Stacey. Reprinted in D. Black, *Theory of committees and elections*. Cambridge: Cambridge University Press, 1958.

Eagly, A. H., and S. Chaiken. (1993). *The psychology of attitudes.* New York: Harcourt Brace Jovanovich.

Farrand, M. (Ed.). (1911). *The records of the Federal Convention of 1787.* 4 vols. New Haven, CT: Yale University Press.

Forsyth, D. R. (2010). *Group dynamics.* 5th Ed. Belmont, CA: Wadsworth.

French, J. R. P., Jr., and B. Raven. (1969). The bases of social power. In D. Cartwright and A. Zander (Eds.), *Group dynamics* (3rd Ed., pp. 259–269). New York: Harper & Row.

Gigone, D., and R. Hastie. (1993). The common knowledge effect: Information sharing and group judgment. *Journal of Personality and Social Psychology, 65,* 959–974.

———. (1997). The impact of information on small group choice. *Journal of Personality and Social Psychology, 72,* 132–140.

Greenburg, J. C. (2007). *Supreme conflict.* New York: Penguin.

Grofman, B. (1981). The theory of committees and elections: The legacy of Duncan Black. In G. Tullock (Ed.), *Towards a science of politics: Essays in honor of Duncan Black* (pp. 11–57). Blacksburg, VA: Virginia Polytechnic Institute and State University Press.

Grofman, B., and G. Owen. (1986). Condorcet models, avenues for future research. In B. Grofman and G. Owen (Eds.), *Information pooling and group decision making* (pp. 93–102). Greenwich, CT: JAI.

Hackman, J. R., and C. G. Morris. (1975). Group tasks, group interaction process, and group performance effectiveness: A review and proposed integration. In L. Berkowitz (Ed.), *Advances in experimental social psychology,* Vol. 8 (pp. 45–99). New York: Academic Press.

Hartwick, J., B. H. Sheppard, and J. H. Davis. (1982). Group remembering: Research and implications. In R. A. Guzzo (Ed.), *Improving group decision making in organizations* (pp. 41–72). San Diego, CA: Academic Press.

Hastie, R. (1986). Review essay: Experimental evidence on group accuracy. In G. Owen and B. Grofman (Eds.), *Information pooling and group accuracy* (pp. 129–157). Greenwich, CT: JAI.

Hastie, R., and T. Kameda. (2005). The robust beauty of majority rules in group decisions. *Psychological Review, 112,* 494–508.

Hastie, R., S. D. Penrod, and N. Pennington. (1983). *Inside the jury.* Cambridge, MA: Harvard University Press.

Hill, G. W. (1982). Group versus individual performance: Are N + 1 heads better than one? *Psychological Bulletin, 91,* 517–539.

Hinsz, V. B. (1990). Cognitive and consensus processes in group recognition memory performance. *Journal of Personality and Social Psychology, 59,* 705–718.

Hinsz, V. B., R. S. Tindale, and D. A. Vollrath. (1997). The emerging conceptualization of groups as information processors. *Psychological Bulletin, 121,* 43–64.

Hollingshead, A. B. (1998a). Communication, learning, and retrieval in transactive memory systems. *Journal of Experimental Social Psychology, 34,* 423–442.

———. (1998b). Distributed knowledge and transactive processes in decision-making groups. In M. A. Neale, E. A. Mannix, and D. M. Gruenfeld (Eds.), *Research on managing groups and teams,* Vol. 1 (pp. 103–123). Greenwich, CT: JAI.

————. (1998c). Retrieval processes in transactive memory systems. *Journal of Personality and Social Psychology, 74,* 659–671.

————. (2001). Cognitive interdependence and convergent expectations in transactive memory. *Journal of Personality and Social Psychology, 81,* 1080–1089.

Isaacson, W. (2003). *Benjamin Franklin.* New York: Simon & Schuster.

Johnson v. Louisiana, 406 U. S. 356 (1972).

Kahneman, D., P. Slovic, and A. Tversky. (Eds.). (1982). Judgment under uncertainty: Heuristics and biases. New York: Cambridge University Press.

Kahneman, D., and A. Tversky. (1979). Prospect theory: An analysis of decisions under risk. *Econometrica, 47,* 263–291.

Kameda, T., R. S. Tindale, and J. H. Davis. (2003). Cognitions, preferences, and social sharedness: Past, present, and future directions in group decision making. In S. Schneider and J. Shanteau (Eds.), *Emerging perspectives on judgment and decision research* (pp. 458–485). Cambridge: Cambridge University Press.

Kelley, H. H., and J. W. Thibaut. (1954). Experimental studies of group problem solving and process. In G. Lindzey (Ed.), *The handbook of social psychology* (pp. 735–785). Cambridge, MA: Addison-Wesley.

————. (1969). Group problem solving. In G. Lindzey and E. Aronson (Eds.), *The handbook of social psychology,* Vol. 4 (pp. 1–101). Reading, MA: Addison-Wesley.

Kenny, D. A., D. A. Kashy, and N. Bolger. (1998). Data analysis in social psychology. In D. Gilbert, S. Fiske, and G. Lindzey (Eds.), *The handbook of social psychology,* Vol. 1, 4th Ed. (pp. 233–265). Boston, MA: McGraw-Hill.

Kenny, D. A., L. Mannetti, A. Pierro, S. Livi, and D. A. Kashy. (2002). The statistical analysis of data from small groups. *Journal of Personality and Social Psychology, 83,* 126–137.

Kerr, N. L. (1983). Motivation loss in task-performing groups: A social dilemma analysis. *Journal of Personality and Social Psychology, 45,* 819–828.

Kerr, N. L., R. S. Atkin, G. Stasser, D. Meek, R. W. Holt, and J. H. Davis. (1976). Guilt beyond a reasonable doubt: Effects of concept definition and assigned decision rule on the judgments of mock jurors. *Journal of Personality and Social Psychology, 34,* 282–294.

Kerr, N. L., R. J. MacCoun, and G. P. Kramer. (1996a). Bias in judgment: Comparing individuals and groups. *Psychological Review, 103,* 687–719.

————. (1996b). When are N heads better (or worse) than one? Biased judgment in individuals versus groups. In E. Witte and J. H. Davis (Eds.), *Understanding group behavior.* Vol. 1, *Consensual action by small groups* (pp. 105–136). Mahwah, NJ: Erlbaum.

Kerr, N. L., G. Stasser, and J. H. Davis. (1979). Model-testing, model-fitting, and social decision schemes. *Organizational Behavior and Human Performance, 23,* 399–410.

Kerr, N. L., and R. S. Tindale. (2004). Group performance and decision making. *Annual Review of Psychology, 56,* 623–655.

Klayman, J, and Y-M. Ha. (1987). Confirmation, disconfirmation, and information in hypothesis testing. *Psychological Review, 94,* 211–228.

Laughlin, P. R. (1980). Social combination processes of cooperative problem-solving groups on verbal intellective tasks. In M. Fishbein (Ed.), *Progress in social psychology* (pp. 127–155). Hillsdale, NJ: Erlbaum.

———. (1988). Collective induction: Group performance, social combination processes, and mutual majority and minority influence. *Journal of Personality and Social Psychology, 54,* 254–267.

———. (1992). Influence and performance in simultaneous collective and individual induction. *Organizational Behavior and Human Decision Processes, 51,* 447–470.

———. (1996). Group decision making and collective induction. In J. Davis and E. Witte (Eds.), *Understanding group behavior.* Vol. 1, *Consensual action by small groups* (pp. 61–80). Mahwah, NJ: Erlbaum.

———. (1999). Collective induction: Twelve postulates. *Organizational Behavior and Human Decision Processes, 80,* 50–69.

Laughlin, P. R., and J. Adamopoulos. (1980). Social combination processes and individual learning for six-person cooperative groups on an intellective task. *Journal of Personality and Social Psychology, 38,* 941–947.

Laughlin, P. R., and B. L. Bonner. (1999). Collective induction: Effects of multiple hypotheses and multiple evidence in two problem domains. *Journal of Personality and Social Psychology, 77,* 1163–1172.

Laughlin, P. R., B. L. Bonner, and T. W. Altermatt. (1998). Collective versus individual induction with single versus multiple hypotheses. *Journal of Personality and Social Psychology, 75,* 1481–1489.

Laughlin, P. R., B. L. Bonner, and A. G. Miner. (2002). Groups perform better than the best individuals on Letters-to-Numbers problems. *Organizational Behavior and Human Decision Processes, 88,* 605–620.

Laughlin, P. R., and L. G. Branch. (1972). Individual versus tetradic performance on a complementary task as a function of initial ability level. *Organizational Behavior and Human Performance, 8,* 201–216.

Laughlin, P. R., L. G. Branch, and H. H. Johnson. (1969). Individual versus triadic performance on a unidimensional complementary task as a function of initial ability level. *Journal of Personality and Social Psychology, 12,* 144–150.

Laughlin, P. R., H. R. Carey, and N. L. Kerr. (2008). Group-to-individual problem-solving transfer. *Group Processes and Intergroup Relations, 11,* 319–330.

Laughlin, P. R., and P. C. Earley. (1982). Social combination models, persuasive arguments theory, social comparison theory, and choice shift. *Journal of Personality and Social Psychology, 42,* 273–280.

Laughlin, P. R., and A. L. Ellis. (1986). Demonstrability and social combination processes on mathematical intellective tasks. *Journal of Experimental Social Psychology, 22,* 177–189.

Laughlin, P. R., E. C. Hatch, J. S. Silver, and L. Boh. (2006). Groups perform better than the best individuals on letters-to-numbers problems: Effects of group size. *Journal of Personality and Social Psychology, 90,* 644–651.

Laughlin, P. R., and A. B. Hollingshead. (1995). A theory of collective induction. *Organizational Behavior and Human Decision Processes, 61,* 94–107.

Laughlin, P. R., N. L. Kerr, J. H. Davis, H. M. Halff, and K. A. Marciniak. (1975). Group size, member ability, and social decision schemes on an intellective task. *Journal of Personality and Social Psychology, 31*, 522–535.

Laughlin, P. R., N. L. Kerr, M. M. Munch, and C. A. Haggarty. (1976). Social decision schemes of the same four-person groups on two different intellective tasks. *Journal of Personality and Social Psychology, 33*, 80–88.

Laughlin, P. R., V. J. Magley, and E. I. Shupe. (1997). Positive and negative hypothesis testing by cooperative groups. *Organizational Behavior and Human Decision Processes, 69*, 265–275.

Laughlin, P. R., and R. P. McGlynn. (1986). Collective induction: Mutual group and individual influence by exchange of hypotheses and evidence. *Journal of Experimental Social Psychology, 22*, 567–589.

Laughlin, P. R., and E. I. Shupe. (1996). Intergroup collective induction. *Organizational Behavior and Human Decision Processes, 68*, 44–57.

Laughlin, P. R., E. I. Shupe, and V. J. Magley. (1998). Effectiveness of positive hypothesis testing for cooperative groups. *Organizational Behavior and Human Decision Processes, 73*, 27–38.

Laughlin, P. R., S. W. VanderStoep, and A. B. Hollingshead. (1991). Collective versus individual induction: Recognition of truth, rejection of error, and collective information processing. *Journal of Personality and Social Psychology, 61*, 50–67.

Laughlin, P. R., M. L. Zander, E. M. Knievel, and T. K. Tan. (2003). Groups perform better than the best individuals on letters-to-numbers problems: Informative equations and effective strategies. *Journal of Personality and Social Psychology, 85*, 684–694.

Levine, J. M., and R. L. Moreland. (1990). Progress in small group research. *Annual Review of Psychology, 41*, 585–634.

———. (1998). Small groups. In D. T. Gilbert, S. T. Fiske, and G. Lindzey (Eds.), *The handbook of social psychology*. Vol. 2 (pp. 415–449). New York: McGraw-Hill.

Levine, M. E., and C. R. Plott. (1977). Agenda influence and its implications. *Virginia law Review, 63*, 561–604.

Likert, R. (1961). *New patterns of management*. New York: McGraw-Hill.

———. (1967). *The human organization*. New York: McGraw-Hill.

Lorge, I., D. Fox, J. Davitz, and M. Bremner. (1958). A survey of studies comparing the quality of group performance and individual performance—1920–1957. *Psychological Bulletin, 55*, 337–372.

Lorge, I., and H. Solomon. (1955). Two models of group behavior in the solution of Eureka-type problems. *Psychometrika, 20*, 139–148.

Lorge, I., and H. Solomon. (1959). Individual performance and group performance in problem solving related to group size and previous exposure to the problems. *Journal of Psychology, 48*, 107–114.

Lorge, I, and H. Solomon. (1960). Group and individual performance in problem solving related to previous exposure to problem, level of aspiration, and group size. *Behavioral Science, 5*, 28–38.

Luchins, A. S. (1942). Mechanization in problem solving: The effect of Einstellung. *Psychological Monographs, 54* (Whole No. 248).

MacCoun, R. J., and N. L. Kerr. (1988). Asymmetric influence in mock jury deliberations: Jurors' bias for leniency. *Journal of Personality and Social Psychology, 54,* 21–33

Maciejovsky, B., and D. V. Budescu. (2007). Collective induction without cooperation? Learning and knowledge transfer in cooperative groups and competitive auctions. *Journal of Personality and Social Psychology, 92,* 854–870.

Maier, N. R. F., and N. R. Solem. (1952). The contribution of a discussion leader to the quality of group thinking: The effective use of minority opinions. *Human Relations, 5,* 277–288.

McGrath, J. E. (1984). *Groups: Interaction and performance.* Englewood Cliffs, NJ: Prentice Hall.

McGuire, W. J. (1969). The nature of attitudes and attitude change. In G. Lindzey and E. Aronson (Eds.), *The handbook of social psychology.* 2nd Ed. Vol. 3, *The individual in a social context* (pp. 136–314). Reading, MA: Addison-Wesley.

McGuire, W. J. (1985). Attitudes and attitude change. In G. Lindzey and E. Aronson (Eds.), *The handbook of social psychology.* 3rd Ed. Vol. 2, *Special fields and applications* (pp. 233–346). New York: Random House.

McLean, I., and A. B. Urken. (1995). *Classics of social choice.* Ann Arbor: University of Michigan Press.

Mednick, S. A., and M. T. Mednick. (1967). *Examiner's manual: Remote Associates Test.* Boston: Houghton-Mifflin.

Moreland, R. L., and J. M. Levine. (1992). The composition of small groups. In E. J. Lawler, B. Markovsky, C. Ridgeway, and H. Walker (Eds.), *Advances in group processes.* Vol. 9 (pp. 237–280). Greenwich, CT: JAI.

Myers, D. G., and H. Lamm. (1976). The group polarization phenomenon. *Psychological Bulletin, 83,* 602–627.

Nadler, J., J. R. Irwin, J. H. Davis, W. T. Au, P. Zarnoth, A. R. Rantilla, and K. Koesterer. (2001). Order effects in individual and group policy allocations. *Group Processes and Intergroup Relations, 4,* 99–115.

Newell, A., and H. A. Simon. (1972). *Human problem solving.* Englewood Cliffs, NJ: Prentice Hall.

Olivera, F., and S. G. Straus. (2004). Group-to-individual transfer of learning: Cognitive and social factors. *Small Group Research, 35,* 440–465.

Olson, M. (1965). *The logic of collective action.* Cambridge, MA: Harvard University Press.

Ono, K., R. S. Tindale, C. L. Hulin, and J. H. Davis. (1988). Intuition vs. deduction: Some thought experiments concerning Likert's linking-pin theory of organizations. *Organizational Behavior and Human Decision Processes, 42,* 135–154.

Otis, A. S. (1954). *Manual of directions for Gamma Test.* New York: Harcourt, Brace, and World.

Parks, C. D., and L. J. Sanna. (1999). *Group performance and interaction.* Boulder, CO: Westview.

Plott, C., and M. Levine. (1978). A model of agenda influence on committee decisions. *American Economic Review, 68,* 146–160.

Regenwetter, M., A. Kim, A. Kantor, and R. H. Moon-Ho. (2007). The unexpected empirical consensus among consensus methods. *Psychological Science, 18,* 629–635.

Riker, W. H. (1982). *Liberalism against populism*. Prospect Heights, IL: Waveland.
———. (1986). *The art of political manipulation*. New Haven, CT: Yale University Press.
Shaw, M. E. (1932). Comparison of individuals and small groups in the rational solution of complex problems. *American Journal of Psychology, 44*, 491–504.
Singh, S. (1999). *The code book*. New York: Doubleday.
Smoke, W. H., and R. B. Zajonc. (1962). On the reliability of group judgments and decisions. In J. H. Criswell, H. Solomon, and P. Suppes (Eds.), *Mathematical methods in small group process* (pp. 322–333). Stanford, CA: Stanford University Press.
Stasser, G. (1992). Pooling of unshared information during group discussion. In S. Worchel, W. Wood, and J. Simpson (Eds.), *Group process and productivity* (pp. 48–57). Newbury Park, CA: Sage.
———. (1999). A primer of social decision scheme theory: Models of group influence, competitive model testing and prospective modeling. *Organizational Behavior and Human Decision Processes, 80*, 3–20.
Stasser, G., and B. Dietz-Uhler. (2001). Collective choice, judgment and problem solving. In M. A. Hogg and R. S. Tindale (Eds.), *Blackwell handbook of social psychology*. Vol. 3, *Group processes* (pp. 31–55). Oxford, UK: Blackwell.
Stasser, G., and D. Stewart. (1992). Discovery of hidden profiles by decision-making groups: Solving a problem versus making a judgment. *Journal of Personality and Social Psychology, 63*, 426–434.
Stasser, G., D. D. Stewart, and G. M. Wittenbaum. (1995). Expert roles and information exchange during discussion: The importance of knowing who knows what. *Journal of Experimental Social Psychology, 31*, 244–265.
Stasser, G., and W. Titus. (1985). Pooling of unshared information in group decision making: Biased information sampling during discussion. *Journal of Personality and Social Psychology, 48*, 1467–1478.
———. (1987). Effects of information load and percentage of shared information on the disseminating of unshared information during group discussion. *Journal of Personality and Social Psychology, 53*, 81–93.
———. (2003). Hidden profiles: A brief history. *Psychological Inquiry, 14*, 304–313.
Stasser, G., S. I. Vaughan, and D. D. Stewart. (2000). Pooling unshared information: The benefits of knowing how access to information is distributed among group members. *Organizational Behavior and Human Decision Processes, 82*, 102–116.
Stasson, M. F., T. Kameda, C. D. Parks, S. K. Zimmerman, and J. H. Davis. (1991). Effects of assigned group consensus requirements on group problem solving and group members' learning. *Social Psychology Quarterly, 54*, 25–35.
Steiner, I. D. (1966). Models for inferring relationships between group size and potential group productivity. *Behavioral Science, 11*, 273–283.
———. (1972). *Group process and productivity*. New York: Academic Press.
Stewart, D. D., and G. Stasser. (1995). Expert role assignment and information sampling during collective recall and decision making. *Journal of Personality and Social Psychology, 69*, 619–628.
Surowiecki, J. (2004). *The wisdom of crowds*. New York: Doubleday.

Taylor, D. W., and W. L. Faust. (1952). Twenty questions: Efficiency in problem-solving as a function of size of group. *Journal of Experimental Psychology, 44*, 360–368.

Terman, L. M. (1956). *Manual for Concept Mastery Test.* New York: Psychological Corporation.

Thibaut, J. W., and H. H. Kelley. (1959). *The social psychology of groups.* New York: Wiley.

Thomas, E. J., and C. F. Fink. (1961). Models of group problem solving. *Journal of Abnormal and Social Psychology, 63,* 53–63.

Thorndike, R. L (1938). The effect of discussion upon the correctness of group decisions, when the factor of majority influence is allowed for. *Journal of Social Psychology, 9,* 343–362.

Tindale, R. S., and T. Kameda. (2000). "Social sharedness" as a unifying theme for information processing in groups. *Group Processes and Intergroup Relations, 3,* 123–140.

Tindale, R. S., and S. Sheffey. (2002). Shared information, cognitive load, and group memory. *Group Processes and Intergroup Relations, 5,* 5–18.

Toobin, J. (2007). *The nine.* New York: Doubleday.

Valacich, J. S., A. R. Dennis, and T. Connolly. (1994). Idea generation in computer-based groups: A new ending to an old story. *Organizational Behavior and Human Decision Processes, 57,* 448–467.

Vollrath, D. A., B. H. Sheppard, V. B. Hinsz, and J. H. Davis. (1989). Memory performance by decision-making groups and individuals. *Organizational Behavior and Human Decision Processes, 43,* 289–300.

Wason, P. C. (1966). Reasoning. In B. Foss (Ed.), *New horizons in psychology* (pp. 135–151). Harmondsworth, UK: Penguin.

Wegner, D. M. (1986). Transactive memory: A contemporary analysis of the group mind. In B. Mullen and G. R. Goethals (Eds.), *Theories of group behavior* (pp. 185–208). New York: Springer-Verlag.

Wegner, D. M., R. Erber, and P. Raymond. (1991). Transactive memory in close relationships. *Journal of Personality and Social Psychology, 61,* 923–929.

Woodworth, R. S. (1938). *Experimental psychology.* New York: Holt.

Zajonc, R. B., and W. A. Smoke. (1959). Redundancy in task assignments and group performance. *Psychometrika, 24,* 361–369.

Zuber, J. A., H. W. Crott, and J. Werner. (1992). Choice shift and group polarization: An analysis of the status of arguments and social decision schemes. *Journal of Personality and Social Psychology, 62,* 50–61.

INDEX

Note: Figures and tables are indicated by "f" or "t," respectively, following the page number.